AUTHENTIC
SPIRITUALITY

AUTHENTIC SPIRITUALITY

Finding God without losing your mind

JOSH MOODY

REGENT COLLEGE PUBLISHING
Vancouver, British Columbia

Regent College Publishing
5800 University Boulevard, Vancouver, BC V6T 2E4 Canada
Web: www.regentpublishing.com
E-mail: info@regentpublishing.com

Regent College Publishing is an imprint of the Regent Bookstore <www.
regentbookstore.com>. Views expressed in works published by Regent
College Publishing are those of the author and do not necessarily represent
the official position of Regent College <www.regent-college.edu>.

Library and Archives Canada Cataloguing in Publication

Moody, Josh
Authentic spirituality / Josh Moody.

ISBN 978-1-57383-403-2

1. Spiritual life—Christianity. I. Title.

BV4501.3.M662 2008   248.4   C2007-901288-4

Contents

PREFACE

This is a republication of a work that originally appeared in England in 2000. It is being published again because, from what I hear, the issues it discusses remain of significant relevance. Postmodernism is no longer new, it is true, but instead it is steadily moving towards being the default mentality of many people. Of course religion is relative. Of course absolute truth is unattainable. Of course the Bible means different things to different people.

At the same time—and as some of us predicted way back in the 1990s—there has emerged a fascination with the "spiritual," or at least the paranormal. We live in this strange bifurcation: The God of the Bible is unfashionable while at the same time it is acceptable to be spiritual. "I'm not religious" (If I had a penny for every time I have heard this I would be a rich man) "but I am spiritual."

So the key task for those of us trying to live as genuine disciples of Christ in this world at present, is both to incarnate and advocate for our faith as the "Authentic Spirituality." This book is not really a work of apologetics, nor is it a resource for personal piety. I hope it does both those things; I hope it both defends the faith and encourages true living of that faith. But it's more like one of those old travel guides you might find in a second-hand book store, which when you open them have a map folded inside to help familiarize you with the city you are planning to visit. It's a description of how the biblical Christian faith is really the most, indeed in a sense the only, authentic spiritual experience.

Paul's letter to the Colossians has long been my anchor in these times. Paul speaks to a church threatened by a subtle, probably early Gnostic, teaching which effectively denigrated Christ at the expense of apparently superior spiritualities. My purpose, reflecting Paul's, is that *you may be encouraged in heart and united in love, so that you may have the full riches of complete understanding, in order that you may know the mystery of God, namely Christ, in whom are hidden all the treasures of wisdom and knowledge. I also, if I may, tell you this so that no one may deceive you by fine-sounding arguments* (Colossians 2:2-3).

As always when one re-reads work done some years before there are many nuances and expressions that if I had the time I would alter in one way or another. May all the mistakes be testament to my finite fallenness, and anything that is not chaff witness to Christ's mercy.

I append thanks not only to the original editorial team at Kingsway, but also now to Rob Clements at Regent College, Vancouver, without whose encouragement this book would not have seen the light of day (again).

Josh Moody
College Church, Wheaton

KNOWING THE PRESENCE OF GOD

I am on a journey to discover authentic spirituality, to experience it, understand it and explain it to others. I not only want to know *about* God but to know God personally. I want to experience his presence. I am convinced that real spirituality is all about him and knowing him and enjoying him. I am also sure that today few challenges face Christianity more acutely than (re)establishing the authenticity of the Bible's spirituality.

I have been working on the subject of spiritual experience for many years now. Questions were first raised for me by meeting experiences in my personal life for which I had not been prepared. They did not fit within my neat theological framework. Since then I have listened to people more advanced than me in the spiritual life, both in personal conversation and by reading the writing of the past masters, my concern always being to understand the Bible's teaching more fully. Along the way I have given various lectures and talks on this subject.

The issue is really about how we know things in general and God in particular. Until quite recently the Western world had been dominated by a rationalistic and empiricist approach to knowing, the product of the Enlightenment as enshrined within science. But increasingly prevalent, both at intellectual and popular levels, is a more non-rational, subjective and relativistic approach to knowledge. The interchange between these two kinds of knowledge in Western culture makes spirituality confusing and belief in God difficult for many people. It need not to be so. There is a way of knowing which does not undermine the gains of science nor lead to a dictatorial two-dimensional world without room for the spiritual and the emotional. This book is all about mapping that way of knowing.

There are many to whom I owe a debt of gratitude for listening to me or allowing me to listen to them. I am especially grateful to my wife, Rochelle, who has supported me sacrificially, and for the gift of Josiah and Sophia who have arrived in the world since the first version of this work. Above all I wish to acknowledge the saving power of the Lord Jesus Christ, before whom I bow and offer up this small service, looking forward with more joy than I can express to the day when I hope to hear him say to me, "Well done, good and faithful servant!" (Matthew 25:23).

SECTION 1

A CHANGING WORLD

*"We are citizens of two worlds, the world of time
and the world of eternity"*

—Dr. Martin Luther King Jr.

1

HOW CAN WE BE SO ARROGANT?

I had been working in Central Asia for some time, and had immersed myself in the culture and challenges of the local area. When I returned to England I got something of a shock. I was in a university bar with some others taking part in an evangelistic question-and-answer session organized by a campus ministry. Things weren't going very well. We had a PA system, but still we could hardly be heard above the din of laughing and talking. And when we made ourselves heard no one seemed very interested.

Suddenly a woman stormed to the front, grabbed the microphone, stared me in the face and said, "You believe in one God, right?"

I thought, well, at least we'd managed to get something across this evening, so I replied rather wearily, "Right."

"So," she paused to think over the implications of this, "that means that you think that all the other gods are wrong, right?"

There were a whole host of things I would have liked to have said about that with a little more theological precision, but, given the circumstances, she'd basically got the point, so I said, "right." Her face went purple. She was livid. "How can you be so arrogant?"

The shock I received was not because the evening was difficult. Telling people about God is seldom easy (though it can be very rewarding); doing it in a bar is incongruous. In a way I expected a rough ride. The shock I got came from *what* was difficult. Things had changed! When we told them that we had good evidence for believing in God no one

13

challenged us or even seemed remotely interested. Even when we told our testimonies of how we knew God no one was surprised. But when it became clear that we believed there was only one God the response was electric. How can you be so arrogant!

Today the one thing that must not be said about your own religion or your own "spirituality" is that it is exclusively right. You are allowed to believe what you like about God as long as you are willing to accept that what someone else believes about God is right as well, even if it contradicts what you believe. When you do not accept that you hit an iceberg of social horror: "how can you be so arrogant!"

What has dawned on me since that evening is that the charge of arrogance leveled at Christianity does not come because Christianity has been tried and found wanting. It comes from a basic presupposition that our society has towards religion. When someone says that Christianity sounds arrogant they are saying more about our society than about Christianity.

I have also begun to realize that this presupposition about Christianity is unfounded. To help you get a feel for what I mean, we need to find out more about the world that we live in. Consider, then, the "map" of the present world in the next chapter.

2

A MAP OF THE WORLD
THAT WE LIVE IN

THE WORLD HAS THREE "LANDS"

We use maps to navigate our way from one place to another, to plan traveling routes, or just to gain an overview of what a place is like. I am not going to lay out a geographical map of physical terrain but a soul map of spiritual terrain. It describes the attitudes of people in today's world.

Maps are useful things; we would be lost without them. Imagine we had a map of the mental world we inhabit, of the internal world of our thoughts. (Of course, a soul is more than thoughts but I mean that aspect of our internal life where we may think of "soul" and "thoughts" as overlapping). What would we find there?

There would be lots of everyday concerns such as getting to work on time or looking after the family. But these important practical thoughts are details, the local Acacia Avenue on a road map of America. What about the large scale, the big picture? Move back in your vision from the avenues, the towns, the highways, back from the counties and the countries to hold in your mind's eye the big picture of the whole world. If you've seen those Google Earth pictures from space, or looked at one of those globes that some people have on their desks, you will know the kind of thing I mean. Now imagine that we could do that with a map of the mental world, where we could depict the big picture. I believe we would see three interlocking "lands." We shall discover that we live at a time and in an age with three characteristic attitudes to the spiritual. They are so well known to us that we barely give them a moment's thought, and yet they form society's basic attitudes to God. They are the religious presuppositions of our era.

1) A land where God does not exist

Nietzsche said it most notoriously with his much-cited remark that "God is dead." Bertrand Russell popularized it, boldly saying among other things, "when I die I rot," thereby attesting to his atheistic belief that this life is all there is. Many others have said similar things. Here's an anonymous letter I came across in a student newspaper:

> Sir—I would just like to point out that God is dead. To be more accurate, he has never been alive. Why then are there still so many people who find it difficult to come to terms with this simple truth? Instead of spending money on expensive organs and elaborate architecture, why don't they spend some on worthy causes? Why not believe in life before death?
>
> I admit the church has been very effective as a meeting place for the socially inept to gather around with other spineless rejects and spend their time idiotically swaying about and flapping their Jesus sandals singing Kumba ya ma lord. But I think the time has come for these sad weaklings in need of an emotional crutch to grow up, assume responsibility for their actions and begin to think for themselves. If they want to follow a social code they should do so for the benefit of society, not just because some God character told them to. Religion is dangerous; it tempts you when you are at your weakest, hooks you, and then slowly eats away at your identity and individuality. If in need of support or advice go to a friend or trained counselor. However bad it is, don't make it worse, if approached by the God squad, just say no.

It would be hard to imagine a letter more full of bile and inaccuracy! Yet it does reflect a genuine attitude that people have towards church.

Most are more polite than this letter, but I guess many people wonder why those "happy clappy" Christians do not grow up and stop believing in "some God character."

The first land, then, is a land where God does not exist. It is a part of our historical inheritance. It is an attitude that rejects the religious dimension. Ours is an age where the transcendent and supernatural God has been assumed by some people to be either non-existent or irrelevant. That this attitude is a fully accepted modern attitude is revealed by the fact that it does not shock us. It is unique in the history of the world. Every other society at every other stage of history has been predominantly religious. That ours has at times not been is probably the most extraordinary fact of the modern western world.

2) A land where 'gods' are fashionable

Oddly, this world that we live in is now developing a rather strange *alter ego*. Dr. Jekyll may be rational and atheistic but Mr. Hyde is becoming religious, at least in some sense of the word. In the 1960s there was significant counter-cultural interest in Eastern religions, alternative medicine and anything "spiritual." That flower-power generation has far from died out. Perhaps in reaction against the rank materialism of the 1980s there is a renewed interest in spirituality. It is not found just in the weird and wonderful sections of our bookshops, nor just in the nether regions of the Green movement, but in the mainline gurus of our generation. Guru may soon not be a metaphor.

Take Douglas Coupland, for example, who coined the phrase "Generation X" to describe those up-and-coming youngsters who not only watched *Wayne's World* but found it funny. Those hang loose, no commitment, cynical in a cynical-kind-of-way people. He wrote another book after his *Generation X* barnstormer, called *Life after God*. At one point in it he said this:

> Some facts about me: I think I am a broken person. I seriously
> question the road my life has taken and I endlessly rehash the com-
> promises I have made in my life. I have an insecure and vaguely

crappy job with an amoral corporation so that I don't have to worry about money. I put up with halfway relationships so as not to have to worry about loneliness. I have lost the ability to recapture the purer feelings of my younger years in exchange for a streamlined narrow-mindedness that I assumed would propel me to 'the top.' What a joke . . .

Now—here is my secret:

I tell it to you with an openness of heart that I doubt I shall ever achieve again, so I pray that you are in a quiet room as you hear these words. My secret is that I need God—that I am sick and can no longer make it alone. I need God to help me give, because I no longer seem capable of giving; to help me be kind, as I no longer seem capable of kindness; to help me love, as I seem beyond being able to love.[1]

Wow! Who would have thought it? Coupland seems to be saying he needs God. When people achieve openness of heart they increasingly recognize the need for some kind of spirituality.

The second land, then, is a land where gods are fashionable. It is neither historical nor modern; it is new, contemporary and "post-modern." The word *postmodern* is a disputed technical term to describe some of these changes. *Modern* concerns for the victory of science and truth have been replaced with "postmodern" concerns for feeling and spirituality, where there are many truths rather than absolute truth, and where the spiritual is far from being defeated by the advance of modern science is rampant and popular. If the rejection of the religious dimension was the most extraordinary fact of the modern world, the return of the spiritual dimension is the most unexpected fact of the postmodern world.

3) A land called confusion

Only marginally less of a page-turner than the sex chapter in a book on relationships is the section on revival and spiritual manifestations in

---

1. Douglas Coupland, *Life After God* (Touchstone Books, 1995).

a book on spiritual experience. But as with sex the greatest help is not going to be instructions of the "how far can you go" kind, or insights like "what's on a man's mind" to enlighten the woman in your life, but the construction of a mental framework to help us form good habits. We must understand why we are confused before we can become clear. We must work out how we may experience God before we can expect God to renew our experience of him.

The prevalence of such spiritual confusion can be illustrated by two examples from the Christian church. The first comes in a paragraph taken from a book by Hank Hanegraaf, called *Counterfeit Revival.* Hanegraaf is concerned that certain new movements promising spiritual revival are delusions. He writes:

> Leaders of the Counterfeit Revival have peppered their preaching and practice with fabrications, fantasies, and frauds, seemingly unaware of their profound consequences. Many of the followers who at first flooded into Counterfeit Revival 'power centers' have become disillusioned and have now slipped through the cracks into the kingdom of the cults. They no longer know what to believe or whom to trust and secretly fear that the untrustworthiness of those who claim to be God's representatives translates into the untrustworthiness of God himself. When selling and sensationalism have become more tantalizing than truth, the very fabric of our faith is compromised . . .
>
> Today's hypnotists not only operate in carnivals and communes, they also operate in churches. What was once relegated to ashrams of cults is now replicated at the altars of churches. Whether they are referred to as Hindu gurus or Holy Ghost bartenders, the methods they employ have much in common. They all work subjects into altered states of consciousness, use peer pressure to conform them to predictable patterns, depend heavily on arousing people's expectations, and abuse the power of suggestion to make subjects willing to accept virtually anything that enters their minds . . .[2]

---

2. Hank Hanegraaf, *Counterfeit Revival* (Word Publishing, 1997).

Compare that with Stephen Hill's description of revival in Pensacola in his book *The Pursuit of Revival*:

> At the time of this writing, we are entering the third year of a remarkable revival at Brownsville Assembly of God in Pensacola, Florida. Those of us who have been a part of this mighty move of God have prayed throughout our Christian lives for revival. But few of us really expected to see it with our own eyes. What has become known as the Father's Day Outpouring took all of us by surprise.
>
> Maybe it shouldn't have. When we consider the wonders of God Almighty, the One who called many of us out of some dark and desperate world, an outpouring of this magnitude should be anything but surprising. Still, we are limited by our human experiences and so a revival like the kind we read about in church history seemed, well, unlikely in the 1990s.
>
> The Holy Spirit, however, has a way of changing everything, especially when people begin to pray . . . Through prayer, we have watched in awe, night after night in revival services, as the King of kings has proclaimed His lordship over more than one hundred thousand new converts and backsliders as they come to the altar broken by their sin. Countless lives have been changed as a result of this revival.
>
> I, for one, will never be the same . . .[3]

Hill is not mentioned in Hanegraaf's book but was deeply influenced by the movements that Hanegraaf so strongly criticized.

These accounts simply do not tally. No doubt you could cite your own examples of such non-corroborative stories, whether in movements, churches or individual lives.

The third land then is sandwiched between the two other countries. Like some partners in the European Union they are uncomfortable bedfellows. They contradict one another. You cannot logically believe both that no God exists and that gods are a good thing, unless you are willing to live with a good deal of mental and practical confusion. Such

---

3. Stephen Hill, *The Pursuit of Revival*, Creation House 1997.

confusion characterizes our third land. Some say one kind of activity is spiritual, others deny it. Some say one kind of behavior is a sign of being spiritual, others deny it. Some say one kind of movement is a revival, others deny it. What are we to make of this disagreement?

WE NEED A GUIDE AS WELL AS A MAP

With that question we reach the limits of what our map can do for us. It can describe the situation but it cannot tell us what to do about it. It can show us a layout of the territory but it cannot tell us where we should go.

What we need is not only a map but also a guide. Then we shall know which route to take. Christians believe that the guide we need is Jesus. He is the One we must follow on our subject of knowing the presence of God. The message or "gospel" (meaning "good news") of Jesus Christ is the foundation of authentic spirituality. We shall hear more about this later. One way, however, that we can immediately realize its significance is to see how other people have followed the gospel of Jesus Christ in the past. When we look back we find that the three lands of our age have a particular historical origin. We also find a particular solution was offered at the time from which we can learn.

3

THE ORIGIN OF OUR CHANGING WORLD

OUR WORLD ORIGINATED IN THE 'ENLIGHTENMENT'

Roughly speaking, the western world of today originated in the eighteenth century. Its three characteristic presuppositions about spiritual things were formed in the period called the Enlightenment. The culture then was different from ours: its lifestyle was different; its rules and regulations were different; but it gave birth to our "world."

The Enlightenment was a hideously complex movement. There are Enlightenments in England, Scotland, France, Germany and America. There are early Enlightenments and late Enlightenments, middle Enlightenments and proto-Enlightenments, scholarly Enlightenments and popular Enlightenments, Enlightenments of science, Enlightenments of philosophy, Enlightenments of psychology, Enlightenments of politics. Plus, of course, there are different schools of interpretation of all these different Enlightenments.

THE EFFECTS OF THE ENLIGHTENMENT

However, while the Enlightenment is so complex and so wide-ranging, we can quickly identify its effects. I am not much of a cook but I know a good meal when I eat one. In a similar way, although an extended analysis of the Enlightenment is beyond the confines of this book, we can get a taste of its effects. If, like a meal, I could serve up the Enlightenment to you, you would find that it would leave an after-taste of profound doubt about the possibility of knowing the presence of God.

The common idea that the Enlightenment was entirely anti-religion is quite wrong. There were probably many thinkers in the Enlighten-ment who were Christians, and certainly many who believed in God. But despite this, there is something in Enlightenment thinking essen-tially opposed to the knowledge of God's presence, whether it was recognized as such at the time or not. That leaves a bad taste in the mouth—at least if you were hoping to taste the presence of God.

This bad taste comes from the fact that the Enlightenment thinkers had great confidence in the sufficiency of reason and evidence to enable us to discover truth. Now, to know God's presence is by no means irra-tional, and in many ways knowledge of God includes an attitude that values the importance of reason. God created our minds. This is why many people at the time, and since, have embraced the outlook of the Enlightenment and believed in God. True religion is reasonable, and therefore false beliefs cannot stand at the bar of reason.

However, the great confidence of the Enlightenment in reason and empirical evidence as a sufficient route to truth, originates in a principle of "knowing" which cannot in the long run produce knowledge of God's presence. As the Enlightenment progressed, especially in France, it became obvious that this confidence in reason was really a kind of worship of reason. The logic went: reason alone determines what can be known, and sits on the throne of knowledge. But we cannot know the presence of God if reason is the only way of knowing. Reason cannot be on the throne: only God can be if we are to come to a knowledge of him.

There is much in that paragraph. All we need to consider now is the idea that the Enlightenment is the origin of our world and that there is something in its attitude to knowing which does not produce knowledge of God's presence.

Before the Enlightenment people took for granted that human beings could have access to God. There were different theories in the world as to how this access was possible, particularly as to whether it was something that was gained (works) or given (grace), but that God could be known was rarely doubted. There was a kind of marriage between God as the known and us as the "knowers." It was at times a rocky marriage, even an adulterous marriage, but a marriage nonetheless. The effects of the Enlightenment caused a break up. In the end, access to God was not only considered theoretically questionable but theoretically impossible. The Enlightenment sued for divorce.

Of course this was by no means apparent right away. The Enlightenment, apart from being complex and debated in academic circles, was also something that developed slowly. It was not thrown on the world fully mature but grew out of a seed or principle of knowledge.

1. Locke

The English philosopher and writer John Locke was one of the great thinkers of the Enlightenment. He set the tone for it. He had strong convictions about the importance of religious tolerance and an honest desire to construct a way for us to know things without fighting over them. Picture someone like Einstein writing during or just after a momentous social conflict, as in Northern Ireland or in the Middle East, and you will have the right sort of context in which to place Locke's work. He was writing after religious conflicts had scarred Europe, and he was instrumental in bringing about a more tolerant society and a more reasonable and sensible view of truth.

However, despite all the good intentions and the brilliance of his work, Locke inadvertently began the process of undermining knowledge of the presence of God. He himself believed in God, but he wished to take the sting out of fanatics who had recently caused such grief and pain. In our time it would be like writing to make sure that the mass suicide at Waco, Jonestown, and among the members of the Cult of the Solar Temple could never occur again. However, in trying to take the sting out of the fanatics he also undermined people's everyday experience of God. In saying that that cult had no reason for claiming a bizarre experience of God he was heard to say that no person had reason to claim any experience of God. It was all "opinion" he said, not "knowledge," and as such should be treated as opinion and not fought over. That was all fine in theory (no religious wars or weird cults) but it was disastrous in effect because it undermined knowledge about the presence of God.

2. Descartes

If Locke's good intentions had an unwitting side effect, the work of another important Enlightenment figure (some would say *the* most important Enlightenment figure) had a different but related side effect. The Frenchman Descartes defended the possibility of knowledge of the presence of God in a way quite convincing to many people at the time. He took away everything that he considered possible to doubt, everything that he thought was not absolutely certain in a philosophically rigorous sense. As he sat by a fire in the winter engaged in this massively demanding mental introspection, he at last thought that he had been given insight to the problem of knowing. When everything else could be doubted, the one thing that could not be doubted was that you were doubting that you were thinking. From this premise, his famous *cogito ergo sum* (I think therefore I am), he built a whole framework of knowledge which culminated in knowledge of God.

Again, as with Locke, this work was full of good intentions; and his writing and thinking have been influential and beneficial. But if Locke undermined the possibility of knowledge of the presence of God by inadvertently discounting direct experience of God, Descartes undermined the possibility of knowledge of the presence of God by inadvertently discounting revelation in addition to reason. Everything, he asserted, could be known from his starting principle of "I think therefore I am." The trouble, as people have since shown, is that such a starting point does not, in a logically consistent and philosophically rigorous sense, lead to such knowledge. The effect, if not the intention, of this great man was to assert reason as the path to knowledge of the presence of God. And when this was found wanting, knowledge of the presence of God itself was considered irrational.

Both these matters—revelation and experience—have featured badly in debates and discussions about knowing the presence of God ever since. They have been caricatured as arguments of fanatics (experience) and arguments of fideists or irrationalists (revelation). In fact, neither of these charges is true, as we can come to a knowledge of God's presence rationally and calmly both by experience of God and by revelation.

One of the best ways to understand this is to consider that the Enlightenment standard of rational evidence for a claimed experience and revelation of God cannot be met by any truth claim whatsoever. The Enlightenment standard is a high-jump bar set too high for all kinds of knowledge, and not just spiritual knowledge. To stick rigorously to that standard leads in the end to complete skepticism and relativism about everything, to doubting your own existence and even to saying that whether murder is wrong or not is simply a matter of opinion. If the Enlightenment standard leads to nonsense we have every reason to think that it is not a good standard by which to judge the possibility of knowing God.

But before we assume that such comparative arguments provide an open-and-shut case against that Enlightenment standard, we need to see that the Enlightenment was not finalized by Locke and Descartes and their followers but by Immanuel Kant. He crystallized the thinking of the Enlightenment and passed its philosophy down to the next generation. In his work the skeptical tendency that the Enlightenment carried in its wake was countered, but only by drawing a curtain across the theoretical possibility of access to God.

3. Kant

Kant's contribution to the formation of the modern mindset cannot be underestimated. You may not have heard of him; no matter, you have been influenced by his ideas. His was the kind of influence that works by diffusion. He stood on no soapboxes and used no publicity techniques but nevertheless his thought has filtered down through modern western society more pervasively than that of most others. It is the quality of his ideas rather than the packaging of them that has exerted influence. To understand our world fully, we need to *read* and *understand* him, especially his *Critique of Pure Reason*. I emphasize read and understand; for those who are bold enough to mention him few have read him, and of those who have read him fewer still understand him.

Whether I understand him or not, I have read him. What makes him difficult to grasp is partly that he was a philosophical genius, partly that he wrote in a tortuous style which is difficult to translate, but mostly that he is involved in an elaborate conversation. Most people who read him have the experience of listening to one side of a conversation, like when we are in a room and you hear someone taking on the phone; all you hear is the occasional "yes," or "oh I see," or "no I would not say that," and of course it does not make a lot of sense. Kant's conversation is with Western philosophy as a whole and especially with the skeptical state that it found itself in at the end of the Enlightenment. To hear his voice one has to be able to hear these other voices as well.

What Kant says is essentially this: Yes, I agree that absolute knowledge is doubtful. Yes, I agree that absolute knowledge of God is impossible. But I do not think that means that I cannot believe in truth or God. Why? Because though I cannot have access to God or truth in absolute terms, I can have access to their appearance. What Kant means by "appearance" is difficult, but understanding his distinction between God as he is and God as he appears is much less important than the fact that Kant makes the distinction at all. In other words, Kant drew a curtain across the possibility of absolute access to God and truth and counseled us to be content with an *appearance* of God and truth, because that is all that is possible. The Enlightenment sued for divorce; Kant made the divorce settlement as comfortable as possible. So the contemporary world considers that knowledge of God is irrational and impossible, but knowledge itself is viable and useful. This is the crucial issue. It means that our three characteristics of the world's attitude to religion are not ultimately going to be tackled satisfactorily until we have solved the basic problem of how to get knowledge of God. The problems of elementary belief in God, of the rise of spiritualities, and the spiritual confusion of the church, revolve around this one issue of access to God.

THE ENLIGHTENMENT AFFECTS OUR WORLD

We can see how this attitude toward knowledge of God has affected the constitution of all three "lands" of our world.

Atheists, by and large, are not impressed with arguments for the historical reliability of the Bible, or even the logical likelihood of God as shown by the construction of nature. To many people these matters seem established beyond reasonable doubt. But an atheist does not usually think that proof of the existence of God is possible. The evidence cannot be good enough because he or she holds the Enlightenment view that God cannot be known.

Or take someone who is instead very interested in spiritual things of all kinds. They are as interested, say, in Buddha as in Jesus, in the Dalai Lama as the Pope. Such a person finds the idea of exclusive loyalty to Jesus (or to the Pope for that matter) difficult to swallow, partly because of the Enlightenment idea that God cannot be known—to claim that you know God exclusively is therefore a mistake.

Or take the confusion of the third land. Why is there so much disagreement about whether this or that set of spiritual experiences is true or false? No doubt personal preference, difficult standards of testing and other reasons could be suggested, but the crucial cause of confusion is that we live with a basic cultural attitude that God cannot be known. With that attitude unchallenged, we have no divine fixed point against which to assess spiritual experiences. We may be able to agree that certain experiences are interesting and useful but if God cannot be known we shall remain confused about whether they are true or false.

28

We need a satisfying solution to the problem of knowing the presence of God. Each of our lands poses a question about knowledge of God. The first land asks whether God exists, the second asks which God exists and the third asks what a real experience of God is. Answers to each of these three questions will be put forward in the three sections of this book: The Existence of God (does God exist?), The Salvation of Christ (which God?), and the Experience of the Spirit (what is real spiritual experience?).

Fortunately, we are not alone in tackling this problem of knowing God's presence. People prior to us have attempted to meet the demands of our world's mindset. One in particular noted the birth of our modern world in the Enlightenment and responded with a contrary gospel enlightenment. Although he does not supply us with all the answers, he does give us a feel for the kind of answer we need.

4

A SOLUTION OFFERED

GOSPEL ENLIGHTENMENT

This enlightenment is not that of the eighteenth century but of the light of the Christian gospel. At the Enlightenment crossroads of history, one voice, little listened to at the time and little understood since, stood on the frontiers of society and called our world back to its senses. By no means everything he said was right (he was only human after all) but his approach was the right one: to actively respond with a gospel enlightenment to the source of our world's basic attitude to religion formed by the Enlightenment.

His name was Edwards, Jonathan Edwards. Apologies for introducing him like James Bond, but he has been regarded as the cure-all for spiritual ills in some Christian circles. An agent with a kind of license to heal. I would not want to stop anyone from reading him, because he really does have a lot to say, but the first thing to learn from him is that we should not learn too much from him.

1. Edwards refounded our world by the Bible.

In other words, he was different than many of his contemporaries because he determined to look for answers primarily in the revelation that God had given in Jesus Christ as recorded in the Scriptures. If we are to listen to him we should do likewise, and not get so enamored with him that we listen primarily to him and not to the Bible. Nothing would have appalled Edwards more.

This biblical focus is found partly in his personal discipline. One of his friends described him as someone who delighted above all in the study of the Bible, and who spent more time in such activity than most other theologians and pastors with whom he was acquainted. His rigorous concern to be biblical cannot be missed in his copious private notebooks on various theological themes.

But more importantly, as a result of his biblical emphasis, he believed that the right way to think was to think God's thoughts after him. It could be said that he did not so much submit his reason to revelation as to reason after revelation. He was simply not willing to submit his reason to revelation in the sense that "God knows more than I do." He considered that more accurate and dynamic relation between reason and revelation came from the willingness to think after the Bible; in other words, to follow its course.

2. Edwards refounded our world not by "rationalism" nor by "emotionalism" but by the "heart."

Edwards said that it was important to understand that God's way of revealing himself could be grasped neither solely by reason nor solely by emotion. Instead, when rightly reasoned and rightly felt, knowledge of God would combine both reason and emotion in the "heart." That is not how we use the word 'heart' these days, meaning our romantic attachments or emotional affections. The Bible uses the word in its ancient Hebrew sense of being the junction of my thinking and feeling; what I have a heart for is what I desire, want with all my thinking and feeling—with all my heart.

Other responses to the challenges of the Enlightenment were more common. We shall look at some of them in the section on "The Experience of the Spirit." Edwards was set apart from some of his contemporaries by the "heart" experience he believed the Bible taught.

3. Edwards refounded our world neither by incorporating nor ignoring new scientific discoveries, but by reforming them.

I use the word "reform" with considerable care owing to its loaded case history. It is associated with the continental Reformers Luther and Calvin, with the Reformation and the beginning of Protestantism. I intend to make that association. Edwards did not abandon his heritage as a reformed and evangelical Protestant in the face of the new science. Neither, though, did he bury his head in the sand ostrich-like and ignore the threats and challenges the new science paid to Christianity. Instead, he attempted to reform them, to rework them, to bring these discoveries into line with what he took to be biblical revelation.

Many other Christians at the time were fascinated by the new science. Edwards was far from alone in being interested in it and positive towards it. We—who live on the other side of the later Darwinian developments of the new science and the media-inspired idea that science is locked in cosmic battle with religion for the soul of society—have difficulty grasping this. Edwards, though, was unusual in not only welcoming the new science, but seeing where it was a threat to Christianity, and then attempting to meet that threat on biblical grounds.

4. Edwards refounded our world in a galaxy where God's presence could be known.

Edwards has often been heard in rather brutal monotone. In other words, people who have read him have tended only to read some of him, and those who have read more of his numerous writings have tended to conclude that there is a basic disharmony in Edwards. For many this disharmony lies in the evidently different tone he employs in his preaching and in his private notebooks; the former is bold and evangelical, the latter questioning and modern. So some readers conclude that Edwards was a split personality, who inwardly desired to reject the shackles of his outdated evangelical dogma and to embrace radical digressions of modern thinking recorded in his notebooks. Poor Edwards, in other words. But Edwards was not such a split personality and his two voices were far from being contrary. They actually operated in harmony, in glorious stereo. Edwards had a consistent vision to describe a world where the possibility of knowing God was not ludicrous but sensible, available, and inevitable.

His aim was to preach and write, to form a world view in contra-distinction to the Enlightenment world developing around him. His was a world where access to the Ultimate was real and necessary and personal. God could be known. His presence could be felt. This was an attempted refoundation of the modern world in a different galaxy, not of darkness but of gospel enlightenment.

Whether Edwards succeeded or not is a matter for the historians to decide. We know this at least, though: the problems he diagnosed are still with us and to that extent he failed. But he showed the way of success, a way not without difficulty and trauma, bringing our world into the light of the gospel of Jesus Christ.

To that end we now turn. Our goal is to convey to our experience of reality a consciousness of the presence of the living God. We want to know that he exists, we want to know who he is, and we want to know his presence. Our task is to see how we may gain access to God, how we may know the real "God" and how we may be sure what is a true experience of God.

Breathe a silent prayer. We are asking God to reveal his glory in this, our contemporary, world. We are asking to know his presence.

Is this arrogant? Some people say it is. But what else can we do? For two thousand years now the following prophecy has stood completed: "All this took place to fulfill what the Lord had said through the prophet: 'The virgin will be with child and will give birth to a son, and they will call him Immanuel'—which means, 'God with us'" (Matthew 1:22–3).

We do not live in a land devoid of God's existence, nor in a land where gods are fashionable, nor in a land of spiritual confusion, but in Immanuel's land, a place where God is with us. There is a true land and our maps need to conform to it.

THE EXISTENCE OF GOD

The fool says in his heart, "There is no God."
Psalm 14:1

5

IT'S ABOUT FAITH

People find "faith" difficult to accept. For some the idea of "believing" something, as opposed to reasoning it, is abhorrent. Others would like to believe in God but just don't seem to be able to. Such difficulties that people have with the concept of faith need to be surmounted if genuine belief in the existence of God is to be generated. The rest of this section will be dealing with this and related issues to the existence of God.

We need to clarify our terms because the word *faith* is used in widely divergent ways. As a result it has almost become a vacuum word, devoid of meaning in the sense of precise definition, but surrounded by atmosphere and intrigue. For instance, the way the word *faith* is used in the expression "faith-healer" is a million miles away from its use in the expression "the Christian faith." One is basically subjective in connotation, relating to the power of positive thinking and such; the other is basically objective, relating to doctrine and creeds. Spiritual misdirection can result from this confusion of terms. People can be counseled to "just believe," as if there were something virtuous in the faith itself irrespective of its object. Alternatively, we can be taught "the faith" as a system of beliefs as if once we have understood it, we inevitably "believe."

I propose to define faith in a more dynamic and normal way than either of these polarized interpretations.

Faith is more normal than these interpretations in that it is not distinctly religious. We all exercise faith in our everyday lives. When we sit on a chair we are putting our faith in it to support our weight. When we fly in an airplane we are putting our faith in the pilot. When we make friends we are putting our faith in a relationship. Faith is not weird; it is the normal human psychological mechanism of mental appropriation. In this sense it is more like trust. And while at times we may have good reason to be cynical about life, without trust we risk remaining in a permanent limbo land of indecision and alienation.

Faith is more dynamic than these interpretations in that while it involves everyday trust, belief in God is "supernatural," it goes beyond the natural. It is supernatural in its reference (God is Spirit) and in its reception (it is a gift from God). There is a kind of spiritual dynamism to faith that cannot be catalogued and pinned down by its very nature. Only a dead faith can be dissected. Faith is chosen and choosing, gift and decision, grace and action.

As we unpack this definition of faith we shall see how we can believe in the existence of God. First, we need to turn to the Bible in order to hear what it says about knowing the existence of God. Second, we need to get into conversation with others who have thought deeply about the matter in the past to learn from them. And finally, we shall propose an approach to dealing with current doubts about the existence of God.

6

KNOWING IN THE BIBLE

We all realize there is more than one way of knowing: mathematical knowing, scientific knowing, and relational knowing, among others. It is important to be aware of which kind of knowing we are dealing with in any particular situation. A wife will not be pleased if she asks her husband, "Do you love me?" and he replies with a statement of mathematical probability. One the other hand, a math teacher will not be pleased if he asks a pupil to show his work and he replies, "I just know it's right." In each situation an incorrect response is made because the wrong kind of knowing is employed. Blaise Pascal may have been right when he said that "the heart has its reasons that reason knows not," but math has it the other way around.

When we think about knowing that God exists many of us are confused because we approach the subject with the wrong kind of knowing. The Bible advances a particular kind of knowing, which we might technically call an "epistemology of the spiritual."

Being unaware of this is like being ignorant of math in the math room or ignorant of love in the bedroom. And because our society as a whole has adopted a way of knowing that is foreign to that which the Bible assumes, we are in that kind of embarrassing situation. Christians can be as enthusiastic as they like about God but it all seems distant and foreign to this world where God is such a stranger.

Our world accepts the validity of a rationalistic way of knowing ("math") and another way that is emotional ("love"), as long as each is contained within its respective sphere. However, the Bible's way of knowing is neither of these, even though its knowing is all-encompassing. Some scholars have tried to make the Bible more like math and examined it for formal proofs of the existence of God. Others have tried to make it more like love and interpreted the Bible mystically. Both have elements of truth in them. The Bible is a kind of love letter from God and it does treat its readers as rational beings. But neither approach gives the full picture.

THE LAND WHERE PEOPLE DO NOT BELIEVE IN GOD

Here we come to investigate the territory of the first land we talked about in the first section: the land where people do not believe in God. What does the Bible have to say about this state of atheism? At first glance, of course, the most noticeable thing is that the Bible does not have very much to say about it. It is not a book written to prove the existence of God but to proclaim the Word of God. It is not a philosophical (or even theological) treatise. It is, Christians believe, God speaking. Does that mean then that the Bible really has nothing to say to those who struggle to accept the existence of God? I think not. Actually I think it has much help to offer. The case it makes in answer to the philosophy of atheistic materialism is a very strong one. To see this we need to see several things at once and to hold them in our mind together and reflect upon their meaning and consequences.

1. God is not hiding.

The first thing we need to see is that the Bible makes it quite clear that God is not hiding. He has revealed himself, the Bible says, not only in the Bible, but also in nature. That means he shows himself in what is normally called the "natural world," as well as in the human psyche and society. There is no place where God's voice is not heard. As the psalmist says, "The heavens declare the glory of God . . . . Their voice goes out into all the earth . . . ." (Psalm 19:1–4). This "general revelation," as the theologians call it, is why the apostle Paul is confident that

40

we are all responsible for what we believe about God. God's "invisible qualities" have been made "visible" in nature—this is a lesser revelation than that in the Bible and Jesus but it is sufficient to mean that we are all "without excuse" (Romans 1:20). Everyone, therefore whether they read the Bible or not, has a responsibility to God, "For God does not show favoritism" (Romans 2:11); he is not hiding.

2. There is enough evidence.

The second thing we need to see is that if someone does not accept the evidence of God it is not because there is not enough evidence. The renowned atheist Bertrand Russell once remarked that if after he died he found out there was a God he would excuse his unbelief by saying "not enough evidence, God, not enough evidence." But if the Bible is accurate in claiming that God's voice is heard throughout nature, this excuse cannot be a good one. There must be plenty of evidence. Why, then, did Russell and others think otherwise? Perhaps one of the most profound places where the Bible analyzes the reason for this is in the first verse of Psalm 14. Here it depicts the atheist as a person who "says in his heart 'there is no God'" and diagnoses him a "fool." Now the Psalm is not calling this person stupid. Of course there have been intelligent people who have denied God's existence. It is claiming that such a person has spiritually suppressed or denied the evidence. He has said "no" in his "heart." In this sense atheists are fools, foolish because they have refused to accept the evidence.

3. Knowledge is by faith.

Now, this seems hard teaching perhaps. But before coming to the conclusion that the Bible is prejudiced, we should consider the third thing we need to see: that the Bible tells us salvation is by faith alone. If you have studied history you will know that the Western church divided in the sixteenth century over this one word "alone." The Reformers believed strongly that we are not really saved by faith if it is faith plus works that save us, hence the slogan "faith alone." But the point I am making here is one that any Christian would agree with. Paul tells us in his letters that being saved involves trusting God many times and in many different ways. Here we might consider Paul's letter to the Romans. But it is not just in Romans. Elsewhere Paul also says that we are saved "by faith in Jesus Christ" (Galatians 2:16). And not just Paul; Jesus too urges us to "Repent and believe the good news" (Mark 1:15).

If we can hold all these three things in our mind at once I think we shall see what the Bible has to say about atheism. It tells us that God has shown himself everywhere incontrovertibly, that we are rebellious fools if we still say he does not exist, and that salvation is by faith alone. What is the inevitable conclusion about the land where people say God does not exist? It is that we can only accept God's existence by faith.

WHERE DOES REASON FIT IN?

I want to clarify what I am saying and what I am not saying. I am not saying that the Bible does not present reasons for the existence of God, or that there are not good reasons for the existence of God, or that we shouldn't be concerned with these reasons. Far from it. There are many places where the Bible argues for the existence of God and the arguments are logically sound.

The Bible argues from *nature* when presented with people who are unfamiliar with the Scriptures.

> Yet he [God] has not left himself without testimony: He has shown kindness by giving you rain from heaven and crops in their seasons; he provides you with plenty of food and fills your hearts with joy. (Acts 14:17)

> God did this so that men would seek him and perhaps reach out for him and find him, though he is not far from each one of us. (Acts 17:27)

The Bible argues from the *Old Testament* when presented with Jewish people:

No, this is what was spoken by the prophet Joel: "In the last days, God says, I will pour out my Spirit on all people." (Acts 2:16–17)

We tell you the good news: What God promised our fathers he has fulfilled for us, their children, by raising up Jesus. As it is written in the second Psalm: "You are my Son; today I have become your Father." (Acts 13:32–3)

And the apostles argue first and foremost that we can know the truth of Christianity because of the historical event of the *resurrection of Jesus:*

God has raised this Jesus to life, and we are all witnesses of the fact. (Acts 2:32)

But the one whom God raised from the dead [Jesus] did not see decay. Therefore, my brothers, I want you to know that through Jesus the forgiveness of sins is proclaimed to you. (Acts 13:37–8)

He [God] has given proof of this to all men by raising him [Jesus] from the dead. (Acts 17:31)

These are the three main categories of arguments that the Bible presents as reasons and evidence for the existence of God. They are powerful and cogent reasons to accept his existence, and I would not want to be heard to be saying otherwise. The argument from nature is now, at a purely scientific level, stronger than it has been for centuries with the advent of the "anthropic principle." This is the discovery that the universe shows amazing evidence of being crafted with precision to sustain human life. However, what I am saying is that acceptance of these arguments is only psychologically and spiritually possible through faith. We can only know the existence of God if we find ourselves able to respond to the existence of God with faith. Does this then undermine all the arguments? If we fall back upon faith is this not merely "a matter of faith" or "a matter of opinion," not a matter of evidence and fact? Not at all! As we shall see later all knowledge is faith knowledge. We can know nothing if we do not find ourselves able to believe it. God is not doing something strange to us by presenting his existence to us in the form we have seen the Bible describe. He is approaching us in the only way possible—through our ears (he speaks), to our minds (he reasons), and for our will (we believe).

CONCLUSION OF KNOWING IN THE BIBLE

As I said earlier, the discussions surrounding being "saved by faith" have a long history to them. It is nothing unusual to hear preachers and Christian commentators saying that people need to be saved by faith. What is less usual these days is to hear people say that we cannot know that God exists except by faith. But I am quite sure this is the inevitable conclusion of the three facets of the Bible's teaching about this matter. There is a definite, though implicit, "epistemology of the spiritual" that underlies the biblical material. Look at the Bible for yourself. Read the material and think it through. Then double-check your interpretation of the biblical teaching by how other Christian teachers have interpreted the Bible on this matter in the past. This is very important because it gives us perspective on our biases and imbalances. We should always be careful that our interpretation does not become skewed by our culture or temperament. Reading the writings of past interpreters assists greatly in this as it lifts us to a vantage point from which to view the Bible from outside our own disposition and time. What did the past masters of the biblical interpretation say about accepting the existence of God? As we shall see in the next chapter, a strong line of tradition makes the same point we have been making. We are saying nothing new, but simply reiterating the Bible's message to those who struggle to accept the existence of God. Treat the evidence for God's existence as you would for everyday things. This is neither math nor art, but is a relationship that requires trust.

7

LESSONS FROM HISTORY ON KNOWING

"The only thing we learn from history is that we learn nothing from history" a politician is alleged to have remarked. If our collective amnesia is anything to go by, he was not far from wrong. Because, while we could learn a lot from the successes and the mistakes of the past, we are often too ill-equipped to benefit from our forebears. This matter of knowing is a case in point. Many of the issues have been debated before. Hidden in the annals of history, for those who will make the effort to look, there is a ready-made map of the pitfalls to avoid and paths to take.

We shall look at some significant teachers on this subject of knowing and then at the effects of a crucial period in history upon more recent proposals.

1. Augustine and Anselm

Augustine is perhaps the most influential figure in the history of the church after the New Testament apostles. He lived in the late fourth to early fifth century. Anselm is less famous but scarcely less brilliant. He lived about 600 years after Augustine and is perhaps the most celebrated Archbishop of Canterbury. Although they differed in various ways, on this matter of knowing they had much in common.

They both held to the importance of the reason in defending the faith. Anselm actually formulated a proof of the existence of God, the "ontological argument." But they also both thought it important to establish what kind of reason was being used. The framework they suggested for right reasoning is one that has become known as "faith seeking understanding."

By this they did not mean that reason was supplanted by faith in the attempt to show God existed. They were not arguing that you must believe without questioning or that asking for reasons for faith is invalid. Rather, they were establishing what kind of reason God rewards with a knowledge of his own person. That reason was for them a "faith-reason," a way of thinking that doesn't *just* begin with faith, but whose whole nature is held in a framework of faith, without which it is impossible to reason about God correctly. All that means is that reason was not always right: it depended *how* you reasoned. Like milk left out of a fridge, reason without faith goes sour.

2. Aquinas

The great medieval theologian Thomas Aquinas did not entirely agree with this "faith seeking understanding" approach. He did not believe that the human mind alone could prove God. The revelation of the Bible was essential for him as it is for all Christians. But nevertheless, because of his own predisposition, and because of influence from Aristotle's then recently rediscovered philosophical writings, he was more concerned to construct rational proof for God than Augustine and Anselm.

So in the midst of his massive *Summa Theologiae* (intended as an exhaustive systematic theology), Aquinas produced a series of proofs for the existence of God. They are sometimes called his "five ways." In one form or another they are still employed by people to argue for the existence of God. There is a fairly simple pattern to these five ways. In general he argues that some experience common to us in reality cannot be explained in mundane terms but needs explanation at a more transcendent level. The five ways are five pegs in the visible with which he seeks to establish the existence of God the invisible: change argues for an unchanged, effect argues cause, dependence argues independence, imperfection argues perfection, and purpose argues ultimate end.

If Aquinas did indeed expect that his arguments would prove the existence of God, then many people since have not found them to do so. Even some of Aquinas' most avid supporters would acknowledge that not all the arguments are successful. The debate carries on.

3. Calvin

John Calvin, the French Reformer, seems on the whole to have followed in the steps of Augustine and Anselm in this matter. For Calvin there was something about the psyche of humanity and its interaction with nature that gave humans an inevitable sense of the existence of God, a *sensus divinitatis*. This is something we all have, whether Christian or not, whether we read the Bible or not. God exists and we cannot escape it, though we may deny it to avoid the demands that God's existence makes upon our lives. Reasoning for God's existence, therefore, takes on a rather different tone to that used by Aquinas.

A striking example of what Calvin meant is found in a statement by one of the most significant architects of the contemporary mind set. He was another Frenchman, called Jean-Paul Sartre. Sartre said in one place: "If God exists I am not free, but I am free therefore God does not exist." That willful avoidance of God's existence is a precise example of Calvin's observation. God's existence impinges upon my liberty, Sartre seems to be saying. He makes certain demands upon me, but I do not want to obey them, and therefore I deny that God exists.

THE CHANGES INTRODUCED BY THE ENLIGHTENMENT

Ever since the Enlightenment the rules of knowing have changed. Thinkers have adopted a standard for accepting knowledge as justified true belief. This standard is technically called "foundationalism."

Foundationalism can be defined in different ways depending upon the discipline to which it is applied. There are foundationalisms of science, foundationalisms of literature, and foundationalisms of philosophy. There is also "strong" foundationalism and "weak" foundationalism. In general, though, we may say that foundationalism defines reliable knowledge by way of a picture, a metaphor, of "construction." Foundationalism insists that a true edifice of knowledge must be built upon a solid foundation. In consequence, this means that foundationalism demands a large quantity and high quality of evidence before it will accept a concept as true knowledge.

THE EFFECT OF THIS CHANGE

At the time of the Enlightenment Christians responded to this change in two ways. Some took on the challenge laid down by the Enlightenment and spent much effort constructing "foundationally" solid evidence for the existence of God. Bishop Butler's *Analogy of Religion* is a good example of this attempt. Descartes' "I think therefore I am" proof for the existence of God is an archetype of these kinds of argument. Assessments of their effectiveness vary, but few think that they were wholly successful. There are even those who feel that these believers ended up compromising their Christian confession; that the Enlightenment was their "Trojan Horse."

Some avoided the challenge laid down by the Enlightenment. These were people who at a more simple level got on with being Christian and preaching the gospel. A group called the Pietists is often said to have followed this course, though to be fair to them they also produced high intellects as well as good models of social care.

One of the very few people of reputation who followed a different course was the Christian leader Jonathan Edwards (see Chapter 4). He reasoned with the Enlightenment, though not on its own terms, by using biblical arguments.

The important thing to note about the Enlightenment is that it was a seismic change to the outlook of modern Western society. We must tackle its philosophy if people today are to believe they can know the existence of God.

MORE RECENT ASSESSMENT OF KNOWING

The significance of the Enlightenment's effect on knowing the existence of God is underlined by the fact that all recent assessments of the issue have been forced to deal with the Enlightenment's conclusions.

Many (perhaps following Butler's lead) have given evidences and reasons for the existence of God. At one level you can hardly argue with the wisdom of such an approach. When discussing God with a real unbeliever some kind of argument and evidence is usually called for. Nevertheless, if our remarks about the significance of the Enlightenment heritage are at all correct, listing "facts" on their own will not suffice. Modern people often feel that arguing like that is rather naive. In reaction, others have tried to combat the modern mindset of the Enlightenment heritage by side-stepping its evidentialist challenge to Christianity.

An influential Lutheran thinker, Soren Kierkegaard, is often said to have advocated a "leap of faith" to cross the gulf of evidence. This is almost certainly a misreading of his argument. He was in fact proposing something rather more subtle and less anti-rational. While there are strong subjective tendencies in his work, his aim was not to advocate subjectivism in the twentieth-century sense (championed by such movements as "existentialism"). Rather, he wanted to encourage personal, and therefore subjective, involvement in the truth of Christianity. Nevertheless, the leap-of-faith idea has taken hold in the popular consciousness. So some Christians do advise unbelievers not to ask questions but "just believe."

Karl Barth, the most widely cited Protestant theologian of the twentieth-century, did not think that we should present arguments from nature for the existence of God. Barth can be best understood as tackling certain abuses of reason current during his training. In this light we can most appreciate his presentation of the need to stick to the Bible, to let it speak for itself, and not get side-tracked into argument.

Cornelius Van Til, another important theologian of the early part of the twentieth century, argued that presenting unbelievers with evidence and facts for the existence of God was to do them a disservice. He suggested instead that we should look at the "presuppositional" level in our attempts to know the existence of God. In other words, we should deal with why people do and do not say that God exists.

Christian experience shows that there is some sense in emphasizing faith as against evidence, in common with these three thinkers. But important as the insights of these three thinkers are, an unwillingness to engage at an evidential level with unbelievers is rightly criticized. It seems to be sailing close to the wind of un-reason.

For instance, one well-known debunking of this approach was put in parable form. John Wisdom presented a story of a gardener who believes that something unusual exists in his garden. This "something unusual" is invisible, intangible, and odorless. He tries all sort of ways to prove that this something exists. As each test fails, he is reconciled with the thought that the something is, after all, intangible, invisible, and without any odor. To fail to construct a test to prove its existence does not therefore change his belief in its existence, because it exists in a realm (intangible, invisible, and odorless) that cannot be tested.

The parable is ironic. We are meant to think how foolish the gardener is for not seeing that this "something" at the bottom of his garden does not really exist at all. Then we are meant to see that the same holds true for God, who is also invisible, intangible, and odorless. If the concept of God, Wisdom thinks, is such that he can neither be disproved nor proved, then, accordingly, we should conclude that he does not exist. Of course, that is not our concept of God. As we shall see, but the idea of a "leap of faith" plays into the hands of this kind of critic.

Currently, some philosophers who have been dubbed "Reformed epistemologists" are formulating a more fruitful approach. They are called epistemologists because their focus is "knowing" (epistemology is the study of how we know things) and Reformed because they may be defending a traditionally Calvinistic pattern of knowing God exists. In some respects their arguments lie within the tradition of Barth, and probably borrow concepts from the other recent thinkers mentioned above. But in another way their contribution is unique and important.

They have made apparent the weakness resident within the Enlightenment structure of how we know things. They have shown that foundationalism does not, on its own terms, work. Others have been moving towards that conclusion but these philosophers may have pushed the argument to the point of no return.

The debate was kicked off in an academic journal with the publication of a famous paper by Edmund Gettier. He proposed various examples which radically undermined the three criteria (justified true belief) commonly used within foundationalism to discover reliable knowledge. His examples were cases where a person has justified belief in something, but can be shown still to lack knowledge of that something.

For instance, consider this mildly humorous version of one of these examples. 1. George believes he is a dog. As it happens, George is a human and so falsely believes this, but nevertheless George has justification for his belief (he wears a collar, eats dog food, and barks at cats). 2. On the basis of this justified false belief, George infers that either he is a dog or his psychiatrist is liable for malpractice. As it happens his psychologist is liable for malpractice, and therefore George has justified true belief for (2) but does not have knowledge of it.

This may seem trivial. If this is the kind of futile mind-teaser that philosophers produce let us cut their funding immediately! However, things would appear different if instead of George thinking he knew he was a dog, it was the President thinking he knew that America was about to be under nuclear attack. In that case the smallest error in judgment might be critical for many people. Or, if instead of knowledge about a dog, it was knowledge about God.

Since "Gettier's examples," as they are now called, much academic effort has been put into trying to find a fourth criterion that answers them or to supply counter-examples. Alvin Plantinga, an American philosopher who is probably the leading voice within Reformed epistemology, took a different route. In a now equally famous paper he proposed that foundationalism cannot work *on its own terms*, that it does not fulfill the three criteria which it itself uses to assess knowledge, and that therefore, as a system of knowing it implodes. Instead, Plantinga suggested, we can say that God is the foundation of knowledge or, as he put it, that God is "properly basic."

The Debate has moved on since then and it will no doubt run and run. The crucial point is that the work of the Reformed epistemologists has opened up the possibility of constructing a Christian and biblical way of knowing the existence of God. No longer is the modern insistence (stemming from the Enlightenment) that Christianity must defend the existence of God on foundationalist terms valid when foundationalism cannot defend itself on those terms.

CONCLUSION OF WHAT LESSONS WE CAN LEARN FROM HISTORY

We can learn from the past that there is good historical precedent for identifying a biblical connection between the pattern of salvation and the pattern of knowing. In making that connection we shall find help with knowing the existence of God and with coming to a fresh sense of his presence in our lives.

We see that faith is crucial because those who were most successful at arguing for the knowledge of the existence of God were those who kept a balance between faith and reason. "Balance," though is a slippery word. It is almost always positive in its connotations (no one wants to be unbalanced) and yet it is also variable in its meaning. What I take to be a balance is only defined by what I take to be an extreme. It may be that we need to think more particularly in "faith seeking understanding" terms, and we shall look at a way of doing this in the next chapter.

We see that being rigorously biblical is crucial because those who were most successful at arguing for the knowledge of the existence of God were Bible people. While they were flexible in their attempts to answer the questions that the world around them asked, they did not allow their pattern of knowing to become shaped by the world's pattern. We too need to relate the message of the Bible to our world but not let it be changed by the world. The Enlightenment heritage with which we live is the current challenge to the church. A way of being in the world but not of the world in relation to the Enlightenment heritage is explored in the next chapter.

8

KNOWING THE
EXISTENCE OF GOD

We have now come to the point where we can begin to work out the
implications of the biblical teaching on knowing the existence of God.
This will help us to be convinced of the existence of God and come to a
fresh sense of the reality of his presence.

Our tactic will be to tease out that connection which we have already
made between what the Bible says about knowing and what the Bible
says about being saved. Being saved means more than simply believing
God exists; it means having a relationship or a personal contact with
God. But the way we accept God's existence is similar to the way we
accept salvation in one respect: both require faith. We shall apply this
to the current pattern of knowing inherited from the Enlightenment
to show how we can know the existence of God today. We need to hit
three targets to know the existence of God. First, we need to see that
our society's structure of knowing is faulty. Second, we need to see that
faith is the root of all knowing. Third, we need to see that revelation is
the key to knowing the existence of God.

1. Our society's structure of knowing is faulty.

To say that our society's structure of knowing is faulty is not a
judgment unique to me or to the church. In fact, the mainstream of
contemporary philosophy concluded that the way society has tried to

establish reliable knowledge in the past is no longer viable. Foundation-alism has received so many body blows from intellectuals' attacks that many scholars think it no longer stands.

The easiest way to see this is by observing the rampant "pluralism" present everywhere. People are loath to say that any belief system is "wrong." They prefer to avoid value judgments in an effort to be tolerant. We therefore end up with a "pluralism" in which competing (and contradictory) worldviews are all considered equally valid. This pluralism is attractive primarily because people think that it is impossi-ble to know what is true about life and death, and God and the universe. The foundationalism that used to offer a system of judging what is right and wrong has collapsed to such a degree that our society is forced not to make judgments. Pluralism is really a product of a failure to know.

This collapse of foundationalism has been going on for a long time. For much of the twentieth century we have lived with a basic attitude of doubt towards knowledge. Most people have grown up with an all-per-vasive cynicism. We are cynical towards politicians, religious leaders, and any cause or claim that seems to demand more than a temporary allegiance. This cynicism comes in part from a kind of cyclical downturn year upon year in our previous foundationalist certainties. The elements of "knowledge confidence" that still survive are gradually eroding as the effects of doubt dig deeper into the subconscious of our society. There are moments when confidence re-emerges as the cycle turns briefly upwards, but the dominant movement is downwards—we doubt whether we can be certain about what we can know.

I remember from my own schooldays one instance that illustrates this long-standing attitude of doubt. We were exposed to a lecture from a professor of philosophy in the hope that it would do us some good. I do not remember much of what he said, but one particular example he gave stuck in my mind:

> Imagine you're in a park. It is a nice day. You're looking at the trees; you're sitting on a bench. But how do you know you are? How do you know that these experiences that you're having are real? How

do you know that you're not actually on an operating table with some mad neurological scientist playing with your mind, sending electronic pulses through your brain so that you only think you're seeing trees and sitting down? Actually what's happening in real life is that you've got the top of your skull lopped off, and electrodes are hanging out all over the place.

We all thought he was mad. What I did not know then was that this was actually a part (albeit an extreme part) of a respectable stream of modern thought.

Not many of us doubt our existence, or really wonder whether our experiences are the product of a mad neurological scientist. We cannot live that way even if it is hard to *prove* otherwise. But most of us do live with a basic doubt or cynicism. We are unwilling to commit ourselves to claims to knowledge and truth because we do not believe that we can really be sure that they are reliable.

What this means for knowledge of God is clinically straightforward but disastrous: the ultimate (God, the meaning of life) is assumed to be unknowable. People who say they know God are inevitably considered arrogant because such knowledge is thought to be impossible. From the philosopher Kant onwards it has been accepted that we cannot know what is ultimate. This developed into a far more radical uncertainty with existentialism. More recently thinkers such as Derrida and Foucault claim that everything we hold to be true and ultimate is only constructed by our culture and language. We cannot know what is there at all, but can only construct what we want. We do not found the building of knowledge on what is true. We construct it out of our minds.

In all, it seems the house of our society's traditional structure of knowing was built on sand and it has fallen flat.

Where do we go from here? A good dose of common sense would do no harm. But we need more than homely wisdom; we need to return to the Bible's structure of knowing.

2. Faith is the root of all knowing.

In every area of life and learning we need to realize that knowledge begins with trust, not doubt. There is something about the structure of our minds and their association with reality that requires the glue of trust to bring mind and reality together.

Naiveté is never a good idea. We should not believe everything or trust everyone. But a cynical attitude that pronounces belief to be wrong, or guilty, until proven innocent is as inappropriate in knowledge as it is in law.

I suspect we see that this is how the world works when we think about it. We do not ask for 100 percent proof of the authenticity of a brand name product before we buy it. We look at the label. We evaluate the shop's reputation, and then make a decision. Business and industry also function (when they function well) upon trust. You may ask for this signature or for that document of verification but nevertheless at some point you take people at their word.

Scientific discoveries happen by "paradigm shifts" (as Thomas Kuhn described them), which occur when the results of careful empirical investigation force researchers to change their allegiance or trust from one framework of knowledge to another.

It is true, of course, that for such life-changing paradigm shifts as acknowledging the existence of God we need more certainty than for buying a new sweater. However, even when we are faced with large decisions our personal life history still suggests that trust is the determining factor.

If I asked what was the most important thing in your life the chances are that you would think of a relationship, perhaps with your mother or father, or your wife or husband, or your girlfriend or boyfriend. There are moments in these relationships when we need to make life-changing decisions. We need to decide whether or not to leave home or to marry, for instance. How do we go about making such a decision? It usually comes from a mixture of evidence, reason, and, most crucial of all, trust.

Imagine two women sitting on a park bench. They are "best friends." One of them is worried because she is not sure that her boyfriend who has proposed marriage to her really loves her. She says to her friend, "I'm just not sure that he loves me."

"Oh why is that?" her friend asks

"Well, yesterday he did buy me flowers."

"Well, that"s good," her friend says.

"And today when it was raining he did come and pick me up from the bus stop."

"Well, that's good!" her friend says.

"And every time he sees me he does tell me he loves me."

"Well that's good! Why don't you think he loves you?

Pause. "I just want him to prove it."

Would it be surprising if the boyfriend in question was finding this stage of their relationship frustrating? After all, she does not *trust* him.

With God it is similar. The evidence that God presents to us of his existence is of a certain kind. It is not evidence in a vacuum. It is evidence of a relationship; that he made us, wants us and loves us. It is evidence that appeals to what a lover most wants to find in the loved: trust. We are not to tell him to prove it, for there is all the evidence we could want if we would *believe* it.

3. Revelation is key to knowing the existence of God.

It is impossible to conceive how God could have given more proof of his existence than he has done (see Psalm 19). He has revealed himself to the world in such a variety of different ways, and in such a compelling fashion, that even if a miracle were to take place before our eyes it would not be a more powerful piece of evidence. This is the unmistakable inference from our discussion.

God has revealed himself in every breath you take. He has shown himself in the very thought process you are using to evaluate this sentence, or in the language you are speaking to refute or accept this statement. There is "immediacy" in these evidences. They are not only to be gained by long argumentation and intellectual discussion. God is not only available to people with an above-average IQ. A long, complex rational argument does not establish his reality. It is the constant revelation of his own person in our functioning and developing and living world, and in the body we inhabit. In my fingers as I type, in your mind as you evaluate, in our hearts as they beat. All this is testimony to God, because it is his doing. In him, the apostle Paul affirms, "we live and move and have our being" (Acts 17:28).

There is no escape from this revelation. There is no possible argument against it because the argument is proof of reason, which is proof of rationality, which is proof of mind, which is proof of God. We cannot run from God, because the legs on which we carry ourselves are moving at his command and by his will.

CONCLUSION

The Bible advances a particular way of knowing as it does a particular way of being saved. That conclusion has far-reaching implications for the manner in which we argue for the existence of God and seek to experience the reality of his presence. Here then are some guideposts in our way of knowing and making God known.

1. Point out our society's faulty structure of knowing.

Often the reasons why we and others do not accept the reality of the existence of God is due to our accepted framework of knowing. To be able to see that much of this framework is inappropriate for any kind of knowledge opens up the possibility of belief in God and a more biblical structure of knowing.

2. Seek to know and make known the existence of God by faith.

The biblical structure of knowing by faith is intuitively appealing. We can readily see that this is in fact the way we function in everyday life. To be assured that God uses the same standard to bring us to know his existence that we accept for other areas of knowledge is both reassuring and challenging. It is reassuring in that God is not asking us to throw away our minds in order to believe. It is challenging because we are not left with a reason to disbelieve in God.

3. Seek to know and make known the existence of God by revelation.

To find out more about this we turn to the next section, "The Salvation of Christ."

THE SALVATION OF CHRIST

Triumphing over them by the cross
Colossians 2:15

9

IT'S ABOUT REVELATION

"Revelation" is a rather flabby word today. It can mean as little as having a good idea in your work or as much as the special creativity of geniuses. The idea behind the word "revelation" is differen as I am using it and as the Bible uses it.. Revelation in the Bible means God showing himself to us (literally "revealing"), not humanity being inspired or stimulated to new heights.

Revelation in this higher sense is basic to the Christian message. Christians believe that God has revealed himself in the Bible, in the natural world, and ultimately in Jesus. The revelation of God in Jesus Christ is the linchpin of the Christian faith. However, when you listen to debates about religion you could be forgiven for thinking otherwise. Revelation is mentioned in passing, but it is certainly not treated as a serious proposition of the truth of the Christian message.

Why is that? One reason is that there are many other religious revelations in our world. Christians may believe that their revelation establishes the truth of Christianity, but devotees of other religions believe that their revelation does the same. We shall be considering this "pluralistic" challenge to the message of Christianity throughout this chapter.

Another reason why people do not take revelation as a serious concept is that they assume that when you talk of revelation you mean something irrational. Quite the reverse is intended here, at least. When I say revelation I mean something that can be shown to make reasonable sense and can be defended rationally. Revelation is not the last resort of a fanatic. Neither is it "rationalism." Experience of the presence of God based upon revelation begins with God, not us. That's the point.

A third, and often unnoticed, reason is that today revelation is considered impossible. There may be revelations of the lower sort, inspiration and illumination of the human spirit, but revelation of the higher category as we have defined it is deemed impossible. This is because society is still living with an epistemology, the theory of knowledge, formed by Kant. As we have seen, he said that no real direct knowledge of God was possible. And so we assume that there can be no contact with the divine in essence, though we may bounce our spiritual desires and ambitions off the ceiling.

However, revelation actually cuts through the barrier that many of us sense between God and us. It is not about gaining God's attention or presence by our own holiness or spiritual discipline. Rather, it is about God gaining us, God showing or revealing himself to us. True revelation is about God coming down, not about us climbing up.

This section is called "The Salvation of Christ" because to understand God's revelation we need to realize that salvation is not simply intellectual, but has a goal. The purpose of God's revelation is to bring us into a personal relationship with him. He shows himself to us so that we might know him intimately. That is why in the Bible the summit of God's revelation is Jesus Christ: he is the person though which we can know God intimately. That is why Christians talk about Jesus "saving" them: he rescues them from being enemies of God to become friends of God. He is the ultimate fulfillment of the prophet Isaiah's words: "'I have revealed and saved and proclaimed—I, and not some foreign god among you. You are my witnesses,' declares the Lord 'that I am God'" (Isaiah 43:12).

This revelation of God in Jesus Christ is unique. No other revelation makes the same kind of claim. It is unique in concept. This is because Christian revelation all hinges upon certain historical events that happened in the public arena. This is not a secret experience that is unquantifiable and untestable. It is an open book. Other claims to revelation are of course historical in the sense that they happened in the past, and they would want to persuade us of the fact. But only Christianity rests its case upon the resurrection of Jesus that either happened or did not happen and which we can test ourselves by the canon of public history. Christianity stands or falls on the basis of eyewitness accounts. We shall dwell more on this later.

But acknowledging that something is unique is not the same as acknowledging that it is supreme. For instance, you may believe that your neighbor is a unique individual but not believe that he or she has sovereignty over you, let alone over every other being in the universe. Christianity claims that Jesus has pre-eminence and not just uniqueness. To understand this we must consider the place where Jesus' supremacy is shown, and that is at his death on a cross. Various parts of the Bible will concern us, but especially Colossians 1:15–20. Before turning to it, however, we need to note just how much religious fashion influences us.

10

RELIGIOUS FASHION

RELIGIOUS FASHION INFLUENCES US MORE THAN WE THINK

It has been said that the plot of a best-selling book must contain these components: religion, crime, sex, and the aristocracy. A witty person has suggested that the perfect opening line therefore might be: "God help me," said the Duchess. "I'm pregnant. Who Dunnit?" In a land where gods are fashionable a religious best-seller would tell us that we are all spiritual beings, that we are all part of god, that spirituality will make us successful, healthy and happy. It would encourage us to get in touch with our inner selves, to become conscious of our higher reality, to "feel the force."

While not wishing to promote this fashionable attitude to religion, I think it is wonderful that many people today want to be spiritual. That desire is a sign that we are made for God, that real joy is found in relationship with him, in spirituality. If we feel, as the rock musician Meatloaf says, that "life is a lemon and I want my money back," fullness of life can be found in authentic spirituality.

It is just that little word "authentic" that is the sticking point. For while I do not wish to be antagonistic or argumentative with contemporary ideas about the gods, I must be honest with what Christianity teaches. If we are to grow in our relationship with the God of the Bible, to come into contact with that spirituality, then we need to square up to the teaching of the Bible that genuine spirituality can only be found when "Jesus is Lord." This is the crucial test that is given for spirituality: "no-one can say, 'Jesus is Lord,' except by the Holy Spirit" (1 Corinthians 12:3). When the New Testament writers call Jesus "Lord" they do not mean that he was only *their* master, that he was *their* guru. They mean that he was the supreme ruler of the universe, the God of the Old Testament monotheistic religion of the Jewish people. The word "Lord" is the common translation for "Yahweh," the exclusive name for this Lord of lords—God of the Bible.

One of the great advantages of the second land where "gods are fashionable" is that people are tolerant. They cannot abide bigoted attitudes to people of other faiths and wish to encourage an open-minded approach to all beliefs and religions. This is a great advantage because so much harm is done by people disparaging followers of different religions. Much of the West has a predominantly Christian heritage and this must not be used to restrict the careers or freedom of those who are not Christians.

So when I am saying genuine spirituality only comes when we accept that "Jesus is Lord," I am not saying that we should belittle those who do not accept this. Prejudice needs to be rooted out; chauvinism is very far from genuine spirituality. But I think that real tolerance can be found when we believe something is true and other things are not true. Actually, I can only be tolerant of something I disagree with. Being tolerant of something you think is inconsequential or insignificant is as much a sign of apathy as anything else. It is love, of course, not tolerance that is the great Christian virtue. And as the Lord Jesus makes clear, this love is to be shown not just to our friends but to our enemies; not just to those who love us in return, but to those who disagree with us;,even vehemently. "Love your enemies," Jesus says (Matthew 5:44).

But despite all these important caveats, the bottom line is that Christians believe that Jesus is Lord. And this means that growing in spirituality, embracing Jesus as the guide of our eternal destiny, entails coming to accept his supremacy over our lives.

This is difficult for us who live in this second land because fashion influences us more than we think. Even if we avoid being fashion victims, we are all creatures of our environment. What other people say or believe has a profound effect upon us. Living in the second land means being surrounded by people who say that all religions are different paths up the same mountain. And unless we make a gargantuan effort to think otherwise we shall think the same. Unwittingly, religious fashion influences us more than we think.

When we read that Jesus says, "No one comes to the Father except through me" (John 14:6), we tend to downplay this clear summary of the whole of the Bible's teaching on his pre-eminence. We turn up the volume when we read his words about love, and turn down his voice to barely a whisper when he says, "I am the way, the truth, and the life" (John 14:6). I suspect we do this whether we go to church regularly or not. Such statements of Jesus' could have uncomfortable repercussions for us. If Jesus is Lord; if he is the way, the truth and the life, then all religions cannot merely be different paths up the mountain. If that is so, what does this mean for my friends and family, or for my beliefs?

But you may have a prior question to those. You may be asking how in the first place we can be expected to persuade people or believe ourselves that Jesus is the only way to God.

The answer to that question is not found in novelty. The original preaching of the message of Christianity did not occur in a Christian climate. It took place where a belief very akin to our "many paths up the mountain" attitude was the officially sponsored doctrine of the state. The Roman Empire disseminated the idea that all religions were valid and acceptable as long as their adherents would say that "Caesar is Lord." The situation in our second land is similar. All religions are deemed viable and valid as long as tolerance reigns. How did the early Christian church succeed and gain so many converts by peaceful means in such a climate?

Their approach may be gleaned from the writings of the Acts of the Apostles and the New Testament Epistles and Gospels. In summary, we are told that they preached "Christ crucified" (1 Corinthians 1:23). In other words, their message was the actual factual historical death and resurrection of Jesus Christ.

It would be a mistake to think that this always gained an easy hearing. One famous archaeological find from the third century illustrates this. It is a drawing of a boy standing in a attitude of worship, one hand raised. The object of his devotion is a crucified man with an ass's head. Underneath is scrawled the inscription "Alexamenos worships his God." It seems clear that a young Christian in that household had preached "Christ crucified" and was being teased for it. The message of the cross, as it was known in shorthand, was something that was acknowledged to be a "stumbling-block to Jews and foolishness to Gentiles" (1 Corinthians 1:23), which covers everyone. The cross was not palatable to the spirit of the age; it was not the equivalent of writing a best-seller with "crime, aristocracy, sex, and religion" in it and obviously rubbed many people the wrong way.

Why then was it successful? We could mention at least three reasons. First, it was successful because the times were right for the message. There is no doubt that for the good news of Jesus Christ not to be yesterday's news is a distinct advantage. And society and history conspired in various ways to be ready to receive the message of the cross. The "Pax Romana," peace of the empire, was a fertile seedbed for Christianity.

The second reason for the success of this message of the cross is that it was honest. To say that Jesus is Lord, in a society where it is common to believe that there are many different paths up the same mountain to God, may appear confrontational. But the openness and truthfulness of being plain with the teaching of Christianity commends the teaching itself as being open and true. Underhand techniques may have short-term gains but they never produce stable growth.

The third reason is one that we shall be considering at greater length: that the cross reveals Jesus' pre-eminence.

THE CROSS SHOWS US THAT JESUS HAS THE SUPREMACY

> He [Christ] is the image of the invisible God, the firstborn over all creation. For by him all things were created: things in heaven and on earth, visible and invisible, whether thrones or powers or rules or authorities; all things were created by him and for him. He is before all things, and in him all things hold together. And he is the head of the body, the church; he is the beginning and the firstborn among the dead, so that in everything he might have the supremacy. For God was pleased to have all his fullness dwell in him, and through him to reconcile to himself all things, whether things on the earth or things in heaven, by making peace through his blood, shed on the cross. (Colossians 1:15–20).

Here Paul gives at least three reasons for believing that Jesus is supreme:

1. He is the image of God
2. He is the cause of creation (by him all things were created).
3. Through his death on the cross he reconciled to God all things (so that in everything Jesus might have the supremacy).

When we think of Jesus' death, we tend to think of his suffering or his forgiveness, not his rule or authority. The Bible, though, wants us to think of both Jesus' sacrifice and his supremacy. Paul emphasizes this by repeating later in his letter that "having disarmed the powers and authorities, he [God] made a public spectacle of them, triumphing over them by the cross" (Colossians 2:15)

This "public spectacle" was not mockery or personal abuse. Rather it means that at the cross God *shows us* (as in a public spectacle) that Jesus has the pre-eminence over religious powers and spiritual authorities. The cross is God's evidence, his public display of the supremacy of the salvation of Christ.

That is all very well, you may think, but why should the cross persuade me of Jesus' supremacy? Why should I agree with the Bible?

The Bible, though, is here (as always) gracious to our doubts as well as our faith. It does not just tell us to believe but also helps us believe. There is a spiritual dynamic to its message that does not dictate the life of faith but nurtures it.

The truth of the matter is that Jesus did live, did die on a cross, and did rise again. I know that there are people who would disagree with this (although I have only ever come across one person who actually thought Jesus was not a historical figure at all). But the evidence points the other way. Whole books have been written about the resurrection of Jesus. One book was even written to disprove the resurrection but ended up being forced by the evidence to support the resurrection. The evidence for the resurrection is remarkably strong. The easiest way to see this is to consider the arguments that people have offered to explain the evidence away. People need to come up with arguments because the early church grew in such a remarkable fashion by simply proclaiming "Jesus is risen." There was no sword here, no forced conversions. People believed in Jesus on the basis of the eyewitness account by the apostles of the resurrection of Jesus.

Some people have argued that the Jewish or Roman authorities stole the body. But this makes no sense because if that were so they would have produced the body to squash the emerging Christian community. If the whole message of Christianity rested on Jesus' resurrection and the Jewish or Roman authorities had the body in their possession they would have shown the dead body and that would have been that. Alternatively, some people have suggested that the disciples stole the body. Indeed, this was the original argument against the Christian community (Matthew 28:11–15).

But this does not really work as a watertight case either. After all, if the disciples had stolen the body they knew that their message was basically a lie. It is hard to believe that the holy apostles were religious charlatans. And, in any event, they died for their belief in the resurrection. They did not shrink from martyrdom because they knew they would be resurrected on account of the resurrection of Jesus.

My favorite argument, though, is the one I have heard called "Venturini's Swoon Theory." This states that Jesus did not really die at all, but swooned. Jesus, whipped in the Roman style, a whipping that alone would sometimes kill; Jesus, nailed to a cross, not with picture-hook nails but large, ugly, bone-splitting nails; Jesus who, to make sure that he was really dead, had a spear thrust into his heart; Jesus, pronounced dead by Roman guards (and they knew a thing or two about death); Jesus, lain in a tomb with a large stone rolled across the entrance, a stone that would take several strong men to move. Suddenly, Jesus in the cool of the tomb revived. He felt much better, dusted himself off, rolled back the stone that would have taken several strong men to move and beat up the small cohort of Roman guards stationed outside. Or, on the other hand perhaps he *quietly* rolled the stone back (remember the size of the stone?), tip-toed past the guards, appeared to his disciples with blood dripping from every pore and said, "Lo, I have risen!"

As I say, the evidence for the resurrection is strong. But for many today it is not enough. Or it seems trivial. For instance, one person to whom I explained the evidence for the resurrection responded by saying, "Many gurus have done this trick too." In other words, whether or not Jesus rose from the dead does not settle the matter for people anymore.

Perhaps you find that the evidence for the resurrection, the Christian teaching that "Jesus is Lord," still seems unimportant. If so, the Bible prescribes two mental exercises to develop muscles of faith. Both, by explaining the message of the cross, to help us to see why it is that the resurrection shows Jesus' supremacy. One exercise is to recognize the reality of "sin," and the other the reality of the "incarnation." We shall consider these in turn in the next two chapters.

11

RECOGNIZING THE REALITY OF SIN

Sin is not a popular subject. It is not popular even in churches. Talk of love and you will have a ready audience. Talk of discipline, even, and many will be nodding in agreement. But mention the dreaded three-letter word and people run a mile. Suddenly the spectra of hellfire sermons appears before their mind's eyes, a larger finger seems to point at them from heaven, a voice booms from the pulpit, "Sinner!"

Actually, however, rightly understood the doctrine of sin is a marvelous release. There are times when being told that there is something wrong is pleasant. If you have spinach on your teeth, a good friend will tell you before you go out so you don't embarrass yourself. An enemy would keep quiet, or tease you for it in front of others, but a friend will gently mention it to you when no one else can hear. Or if you are seriously ill a good doctor will bravely tell you what's wrong when you ask her. It will not be easy for the doctor to help you face the facts, but it will be good practice if that is what you want. Sin is more like being ill than having spinach on your teeth, and a spiritual doctor will gently mention it to you with a good bedside manner and words that are straight-forward and kind.

Getting to grips with sin is essential if we are to embrace Jesus as supreme in our lives, as the One who rules over us and guides our destiny. We have already seen that the Bible tells us that Jesus is supreme for a variety of reasons. We are told that he is supreme because he was involved in the original creation of the world. We are told that he is supreme because he is the image of God. We shall be thinking more about the divinity of Jesus when we come to consider his "incarnation" later. But if we are to recognize, to accept, to embrace Jesus personally as supreme, not grudgingly but joyfully, not momentarily but in every aspect of our lives, sin is where we need to begin. Why? Because sin is the problem to which Jesus is the solution; sin is the question to which Jesus is the answer; sin is the disease to which Jesus is the cure. When we say to people today, "Jesus is the answer," what many want to know is "What's the question?". Well, the question is "How can I be free from sin?" and to ask that we need to know we need an answer; we need to recognize sin.

Without this recognition we shall be confused at our lack of progress in the realm of the spiritual. This explains the perception of Kant's insight about the barrier between God and us. It is true that we cannot reach God, but it is true because of sin. When we see this we shall be on the way to realizing that while we cannot do anything about it, God can.

Nevertheless, this way of thinking flies in the face of strong winds of opinion coming from the opposite direction. Not only is sin not a popular topic, the concept of sin, and therefore the word "sin" that it represents, is sometimes considered virtually an immoral subject. The moral sense of our times labels sin "sinful." It can be very hard for us to recognize the reality of sin.

The idea of sin seems wrong to us because our gut feeling is that everyone can be spiritual if they want to be. As one commentator on the religious scene today says, for many people "all is one and all is God." If that is a correct comment deep down people assume that they can make contact with God by their own initiative. We sense that God is here, that we can reach him, that we can have spiritual dealings with him. Thus the idea of "sin," of an enmity between God and us, seems absurd and is not to be accepted.

The idea of sin also seems wrong to us because the dominant philosophy of education in the West is that people are good. We think that if we are properly educated and brought up our natural basic goodness will surface. The concept of sin runs counter to this assumption—it seems to promote a very negative self-image. Nietzsche voiced these hesitations clearly (if to an extreme) when he wrote:

> Christianity is in need of sickness . . . the actual ulterior motive of the whole of the Church's system of salvation is to make people ill . . . no man is 'converted' to Christianity,—he must be sick enough for it . . .[4]

SIN IS EASILY RECOGNIZED WHEN IT IS UNDERSTOOD

To go any further in our discussion we need to make sure that we rightly understand the Bible's view of sin. Like racists who hate an ethnic group without ever having known an individual from it, there is a danger that we can be against "sin" without having any clear idea what sin is.

The Bible understands sin as a universal, personal and relational offence against God.

1. Sin is universal.

We can see that sin is universal when we consider one of the best-known passages in the Bible, the Ten Commandments, found in Exodus 20. When read very superficially, people sometimes feel a little smug about them; they feel that they have not done so badly after all. There are probably not many murderers who are reading these words, for instance. But there may be a few more adulterers; probably a large number who have not honored their parents; and everyone has stolen, lied or coveted in some way, at some time. Furthermore, Jesus taught

---

4. F W Nietzsche, *The Complete Works of Friedrich Nietzsche*, vol.16, *The Anti-Christ*, T N Foulis 1911, pp. 202–3.

that the Ten Commandments were as relevant to our attitudes as to our actions. He said that if we lust we commit adultery, if we hate we murder. On that standard we have universally failed to live up to God's commandments. In other words, we are all sinners.

It is important to stress that we are *all* sinners because Christians are sometimes accused of being self-righteous. That may be true on occasions, but it should never be so because everyone, Christian or not, is sinful. In fact, the Bible drives the humbling effect of sin ever further into our self-consciousness. It not only says that we are universally sinful in action and attitude, but also claims that we are universally sinful in nature.

In his letter to Titus, Paul says that our "minds and consciences are corrupted" (Titus 1:15). That is, sin is not just about our actions and attitudes; it is a description of something that has gone wrong in the core of our being, in our very nature. The Titus text is not alone in claiming this. In his letter to the Romans, Paul says that we have inherited guilt (Romans 5:12). Psalms and Genesis tell us that we have inherited corruption (Psalm 51:5; Genesis 8:21).

If the idea of inheriting sinfulness seems unfair, it is worth pondering that this is also how God has arranged salvation. To complain that God treats people as "one" in Adam is not a good idea because he also treats people as "one" in Christ (Romans 5:19). Or we may think it unfair of God to judge us for what we are rather than for something we have done. But our natural sinfulness is not the basis of judgment, even if it is the basis of our sinful actions; rather, we shall be judged by our actual attitudes and actions (Romans 2:6).

2. Sin is personal and relational

Sin is personal in the sense that it affects me and not just you, it is something that affects us and not just "them." It is an obvious conclusion from the universality of sin but one that we are often loath to make. I have to admit that I, not just society, am at fault; not just my family, my background, or my friends, but me too.

The personal side of sin struck me afresh when I was watching a film in which a young preacher was caught in full flow by the cameras. He was looking at the packed gallery in the church, appealing to the faces that met his glace. He was preaching about sin. "Do I have to read the hearts of all that are here present?" he asked. "Do I have to read all your hearts?" he emphasized. "Do I have to speak the secrets of your heart in public?" There was considerable shifting in pews as people were faced with the reality of sin in their own lives.

What struck me was that the answer was within his own heart. Of course he did not have to read out their hearts. He knew their hearts were sinful as they knew that his was. They were in it together. In fact, the point of the scene was ironic.

A little later in the film we see the young preacher compromising his profession, acting in ways that showed him caught in a web of hypocrisy.

Sin is also relational. By this I do not just mean that it has socially detrimental effects, though that is true. Each lie we tell adds a little more to the extraordinary amount of confusion in the world. But what I mean by saying that sin is relational is that it is always related to God.

If we go back to our earlier passage in Colossians we are told what happens when sin finds the solution: we are "reconciled" to God (Colossians 1:22). Reconciliation is a relationship term, entailing the ceasing of enmity and the renewing of friendship. Sin, therefore, is also a relationship term, entailing the breaking of friendship and the start of hostilities. When we say we are sinners, we are therefore really saying that we are enemies of God. That relational nature of sin tells us why sin is so important and so serious: it is a breakdown in our relationship with God himself.

Look at it another way. The seriousness of a crime depends upon whom we are acting against in our behavior. If our neighbor kills a fly as she walks past our window we would think none the worse of her. If our neighbor walked outside her front door with a cute little rabbit and proceeded to kill it for her supper, things would be a little different. We might be squeamish; we might call PETA. But if we discovered that our neighbor had murdered someone, we would be more disturbed.

Whom we offend determines the depth of the crime. Killing a fly is not serious; killing a human is very serious. Our crime is that we have all sinned against the God who made us, who cares for us, who is the most wonderful being in the universe, who is infinitely beautiful, who is love. We have offended against him and our crime is therefore very grave.

I said at the start of our discussion about sin that if we understood the Bible's view that sin is a universal and personal and relational offense against God, we would easily recognize it. We may have already begun to sense that, so next we shall tease out more clearly why the Bible's view of sin resonates within us as a description of reality.

3. Sin is recognizable.

There are two ways we can begin to recognize sin that come from understanding the Bible's teaching. First, we can identify and unmask the myths and misinformation about the concept of sin itself.

As we understand that sin is universal we can see that it is not a concept introduced to support a self-righteous moral elite. I know there are people who have used the concept of sin (or fear of punishment) to sustain a religious dictatorship. But rightly understood we can never think of sin as giving us a right to tell anyone else off; sin puts us all under the judgment of God. It does not give us a right to judge anyone else.

When we perceive sin as personal, we can see that the biblical view of sin is not like a childhood concept of rules and regulations. It is much more to do with the psychological scars and complexities we find within ourselves.

As we understand that sin is relational we can also see that sin is not a straightjacket of unnecessary restrictions from a spoilsport God. God is good and wants the best for us. Sin is rejecting the best and taking the worst. God longs to love us and care for us in intimate relationship: sin is being satisfied with dust instead of stars. Understanding the Bible's concept of sin, then, helps us unmask wrong ideas about what sin means.

Second, when we understand the Bible's concept of sin we see it resonates with our own experience of life, suffering and God. Sin fits with our experience of suffering. For example, some people would find the idea of working with an aid agency like World Relief or the Red Cross attractive. Such Non-Governmental Organizations can provide the excitement of travel with the satisfaction of feeling that you are making some difference to the problems of the world. But if this is what we wanted to do, how would you deal with the suffering that you would inevitably see? Of course, the so-called "problem of evil" is an old chestnut posed by all philosophies and religions. Having wrestled with it personally I do not believe that suffering can be answered intellectually in this world. When I lived in a far-flung corner of the former Soviet Union, I found myself submerged in an atmosphere of darkness and oppression. That year was a bad year for the country, and everything seemed black. The faces of the people, the eyes hard with fear, the voices in the streets raised in desperation, these things often come back to me. But this is just a drop in the ocean of human pain. No logical reason can be given for evil, partly because evil is the antithesis to order and good sense. But we must still reckon with it. It is inconceivable to me how anyone can say that people are basically good when they come face to face with real suffering and evil.

Sin also fits with our experience with God. Most people in the world believe in a god of some kind. Even in the secular West only a small minority of people do not believe in the existence of some higher spiritual power. When we look across all the countries in the world over the whole course of history, the number of people who have not believed in some sort of god is so small as to be invisible. Here, though, is the extraordinary thing: in the west, at least , few people are "religious" or publicly show their allegiance to God or claim to know him. Why is that? An explanation of why people believe in God but do not have a spiritual relationship with him is that there is an estrangement between them and God. Sin has precisely this effect; we are aware of God but do not know him personally because we are morally separated from him. Sin resonates with our lack of spiritual experience.

In beginning to recognize the reality of sin we are completing the first exercise that the Bible gives us to see the supremacy of Jesus shown at the cross. We need an answer for sin; our eyes are then naturally drawn to the cross as the exclusive solution to sin, where Jesus is shown as having the pre-eminence.

The other exercise the Bible offers us to build our muscles of faith in Jesus' supremacy is to recognize the reality of the incarnation. We shall look at that in the next chapter.

12

REALIZING THE REALITY OF THE INCARNATION

The incarnation—the coming to this world of God in human form— tells us that only Jesus could provide a solution for sin; the cross is therefore a display of his supremacy. To understand why the incarnation functions this way we need first to appreciate that the incarnation makes sense, and second, to see that this revelation of God in Christ is different from and supreme to other religious and mystical revelations.

THE INCARNATION MAKES SENSE

The incarnation is the Christian teaching that Jesus Christ is both God and man. This does not mean that Jesus is part God and part man, or that he is just God or just man, but that he is fully God and fully man. There is an entire unity of God and of man in the person of Jesus. This is obviously difficult to comprehend, and there have been countless debates about it in the history of the church.

The best way to approach the incarnation is by considering the more general question of the relation of Christianity to reason. No part of the Christian faith is against reason. This includes even something as transcendentally extraordinary as the virgin birth, the historical event upon which the reality of the incarnation hinges.

However, though no part of the Christian faith is against reason there are parts of it beyond reason. That is not really illogical; if Christianity is genuinely the supernatural revelation of God for all people as it claims to be, then we would expect there to be parts of it that we cannot fully fathom with our minds. A good rule of thumb to test the validity of a religion is whether it can fit inside a human mind; if it can we can be sure it is not divine. But another good test is whether a religion makes no sense to the human mind; if it makes no sense we can assume that it is nonsense. Most religious cults operate by persuading people to leave their mind out of it. They tell people, "Do not think; thinking only confuses the issue. You must just believe." Christianity is at times above reason but never against reason and therefore passes both our tests. The virgin birth (and thus the incarnation) is one instance of Christianity being above but not against reason.

In my work in Cambridge I met some of the brightest people of the next generation. They will be doctors, politicians, lawyers, industrialists, and academics. You might think that reason alone could persuade such a crowd to trust in God. But it is not so. The most intelligent people I have known have acknowledged the limitations of reason. What such people are looking for, especially in relation to God, is certainly something that fits with their reason but that also resonates with their personal experience and intuition. They expect God to "make sense."

We can find at least seven reasons to suggest that the incarnation makes sense:

1. I would point to the coherence of the incarnation as an idea: it is internally consistent. To confirm the internal consistence of ideas is an essential step in establishing their truth. If an idea contradicts itself (e.g. if we say John is both six feet tall and 5 feet tall), it is usually either not true or is a mistake. By contrast, paradox is an idea that *appears* to contradict itself but actually would not if we could see the whole picture (e.g. light is both waves and particles). Paradox may be important because some ideas can be true even when at first glance they seem obviously untrue or contradictory.

But the incarnation is not paradoxical: it does not contradict itself. There is nothing inconsistent about saying that God became human. It may be hard to imagine how it is possible, but this is a problem of power not logic. There are logical conundrums which one can pose about God: for instance, the classic philosophical teaser "Can God make something too heavy for him to lift" is a logical poke at the idea of omnipotence. But the incarnation is not open to such charges of logical inconsistency. It may be something we find hard to imagine, but it is not inconsistent as an idea.

2. I would point out that contemporary science does not rule out the possibility of such a "supernatural" event as the incarnation. Science is concerned with the natural not with miracles. People who try to make science seem anti-religious are misleading. It is true that earlier generations of philosophers tried to argue from science that miracles of any kind were so unlikely as to be insignificant for any belief or argument. They argued that what we know about the natural world makes the supernatural so unlikely that no amount of evidence of a miracle can be sufficient.

Many people have been put off believing in the incarnation or any other miracle because of such arguments. But science has changed. In the past, the dominant scientific view of the physical universe suggested to some that we lived in a "closed box" where God could not intervene. However, contemporary scientific theory provides a view of the physical world more in flux. It is much harder to believe that this view rules out miracles. An atheistic scientist (there are plenty of Christian scientists of course) might argue cogently that contemporary science makes miracles, and therefore the incarnation, *improbable*. But no one can honestly say that contemporary science proves that the incarnation is *impossible*.

3. We can note that the incarnation is a belief enjoined upon Bible believers. John 1, Colossians 1:15–20, Hebrews 1 all teach the incarnation uncompromisingly. Indeed, the Old Testament books written

hundreds of years before Jesus lived also imply the necessity of the incarnation. For example, there is the promise of a child born who will be called "mighty God" (Isaiah 9:6), in a passage read at almost every Christmas service.

4. We can hear the opinions of those who knew Jesus personally. He was obviously human and known by his friends and family as such: he was a baby who needed changing and feeding (Luke 2:4–7), a man who cried (John 11:35) and died (Mark 15:37). But as we look into the response of his intimate friends, we notice that they gradually came to an awareness that he was more than human. So Peter concluded that he was the "Son of the living God" (Matthew 16:16), and even doubting Thomas eventually acknowledged him as "My lord and my God" (John 20:28). Furthermore, it is significant that even a hard-bitten Roman officer saw something of the divine in Jesus at his crucifixion, saying he was surely "the son of God" (Mark 15:39).

5. Just imagine how extraordinary such statements would have been in first-century Palestine. We live in a day when religious leaders can make ambitious and self-aggrandizing statements without fear and their followers can ape them without persecution. But for a first-century Jew to call another Jew "God" was extraordinary, as Jewish culture was radically monotheistic. For Peter or Thomas to be able to say that Jesus was God must have required superlative evidence. Such a statement would not have come lightly to their lips.

6. I would point to Jesus himself, and ask you to join his disciples on a journey of discovery to find out who he was. As we traveled together two matters would become juxtaposed: Jesus claimed to be God, and Jesus was a good and great person. No one has explored the force of this juxtaposition more persuasively than the Oxbridge academic C. S. Lewis. In his well known "trilemma" he argued that when we consider these two matters we must logically conclude only one of three things —it forces us to a "trilemma." Jesus was either mad or bad to claim to

be God, or he really was who he said he was. No other alternative is logically possible, Lewis argued. Few of us would want to mark Jesus, the great moral teacher, down as either mad or bad, and if Lewis was right we are left with only one of the three alternatives. We would need to conclude that Jesus is God.

But even if we sit uneasily with this argument, we only have to look at what convinced the friends of Jesus that he was God: his person and deeds. Something about him was deeply satisfying: knowing him was like drinking from an eternally thirst-quenching spring of water (John 4:14). And his deeds exhibited divine power: he walked on water (John 6:16–21), he fed thousands with scraps (Mark 8:1–13), he healed the sick (Matthew 9:1–8), he brought the dead back to life (John 11:38–44), and was himself raised to life after he had been crucified (Luke 24). If the logic and argument of Lewis does not persuade, then at least the person and deeds of Jesus left those who knew him with no doubt that he was the Lord.

7. While we might still find the idea of the incarnation hard to understand, even scientifically improbable, we could be forced to conclude with Sherlock Holmes: when all other possibilities are exhausted, what is left (however improbable) is the truth.

REVELATION AND REVELATIONS

Throughout this section we are seeing that Christianity bases its claims to supreme truth upon the revelation of God in Christ. We have seen that the incarnation is credible as a statement of this revelation of God in Christ. When people say, "What is God like?" the right answer is "Jesus Christ." Or when people say, "I'd believe in God if I could see him," the correct response is "you could have seen him if you had been born in first-century Judea." In other words, coming to believe in God relies upon us exercising faith in the revelation of God. God has shown himself in a variety of ways, as we have seen, but his ultimate revelation is in Jesus. No longer can it be said that this incarnation does not make sense to the modern scientific age; the miracle of the incarnation need not be soft-pedaled in Christian teaching.

In John's Gospel, for instance, Jesus is presented as the supreme God-man in several ways:

1. As eternal. In the first chapter of the book, Jesus is described as the Word who was with God and was God from the beginning.

2. As satisfying. In Chapter 4:14 Jesus says that he can give the kind of drink that would eternally satisfy.

3. As supernatural. In Chapter 6 Jesus feeds 5,000 people with a small picnic and then goes for an after-dinner walk on water. At the beginning of chapter 9 he makes a person born blind see. And then, to cap it all, in chapter 20 he defeats death. Jesus is portrayed as someone who was not bound by the normal laws of nature but acted as if he defined those laws; he was able to do miracles at will, to change water into wine, and even rise from the dead.

4. As claiming to be God. In chapter 8:58 he quite deliberately put himself on the same level as God by calling himself by the name ("I am") and claiming the same eternity ("I am") as God.

5. The power and beauty of his life and work leads even doubters to conclude that he was God in chapter 20. It is apparent that his life and his claims matched.

6. Therefore, John also concludes that Jesus is God. He tells us this in the start of his book in John 1:1 and 18. And at the end,

in chapter 20:31, John tells us that he has written the book so that we might also believe the same about Jesus.

This is the revelation of God in Christ which the Bible tells us in order that we might know God personally; know his presence in our lives initially and in ever-deepening ways.

What, though, can we say about the many different claims to revelation in the world? Most religions make some kind of claim to revelation. How can we possibly agree, then, that Jesus is shown as the supreme God-man by revelation?

First, it is very important not to get confused by false propaganda. While it is true that many religions other than Christianity claim revelation, Christian revelation is *unique* in concept. We can observe the difference in the explicitly "testable" element to Christian revelation. The Bible tells us to test prophets and teachers. The Old Testament tells us that we can tell a prophet by whether what he said comes true or not (Deuteronomy 18:22). The New Testament tells us to test prophets by whether they agree to the primary authority of the teaching of the apostles (1 Corinthians 15:17). There may be some similarities between Christian revelation and other revelations in *content*, that all tend to make reference to a spiritual life and destiny for instance. But this testable element distinguishes Christian revelation in *concept*. It shows us that Christian revelation is a historical revelation. Other revelations certainly happened in history, but Christianity alone is historical in the sense that its truth relies on historical events in the public arena. It uniquely allows itself to be tested by the canon of history. In effect what Christianity says is that the resurrection of Jesus either happened in history or it did not. Jesus both lived as the God-man and was authenticated as such by the resurrection or he was not God. We can look at the documents and weigh up the pros and cons for ourselves. All history is based on records of eyewitness accounts. So is the resurrection of Jesus. There is no arm-twisting of the life of faith here. We are to believe on the basis of what happened, pure and simple.

Second, no one who has rigorously examined the matter thinks that all revelations appear the same. People who say that all religions look alike are not very different from people who say that all people of a certain racial group look alike. Once you get to know such a group, you realize there are many differences in appearance from one individual to another. The different religions say different things—even opposing things—about so many different matters that we are left without the option of saying that they agree. We can not say that they are all "nice," or think that just being "religious" is a good thing, because there is no such thing as being "religious." There is just believing one religion or another. Sometimes it is suggested that this is not the case on the basis of more substantial reasons. We shall consider these reasons below. But for now consider that the adherents of religions are content to know that they disagree. Try telling Muslims that they *really* believe the same as Christians, that Jesus is God, and they will not be impressed. This does not mean that Christians and Muslims have to be antagonistic in their disagreements. Indeed, they should not be. But it does mean that they cannot pretend that they believe the same as each other.

Third, however, when some people say that all revelations and all religions are basically the same they may do so because of a more substantial reason. This reason is the claims of mystical experience. The particular person who says that all religions are the same may well not have had any mystical experiences themselves. They may not even be familiar with mysticism. But the attitude to religions that say they are all the same often originates in a mystical approach.

Now this is a substantial difficulty for exclusive claims to unique religious truth. The experiences of mystics should not be swept under the carpet as the drug-crazed or ascetic antics of the semi-insane. Religious mystics are those who believe they have discovered an essential oneness to spiritual reality. In some way or other, they feel they have discovered that God or Brahman or ultimate truth is one and the same.

This subject has been the focus of much Western research this century. The renowned American psychologist William James conducted a rigorous analysis of mystical experience, published as his famous monograph *The Variety of Religious Experiences* in 1902. In the 1950s Aldous Huxley boosted interest in mystical experience by converting from atheism to Vedantist mysticism, an Indian philosophy that denies the ultimate existence of everything except Brahman. Frustrated by his attempts to engage in this mystical experience he experimented with the hallucinogenic drug mescaline. His experiences under the influence of that drug were published in 1954 in *The Doors of Perception.* Since then interest in mystical experience has grown, becoming popular in the West in the hippy movement of the 1960s and in the contemporary New Age movement. And the debate about the validity and insights of mysticism has continued.

R.C. Zaehner believed that mysticism could be defined into three categories: panenhenic, monistic, and theistic. Panenhenic mystical experience is one where time and space are transcended by heightened sensory experience. Monistic mysticism is an experience of the oneness of all things. Theistic mystical experience is where despite the emphasis on oneness the distinction between devotee and God is maintained. Zaehner has been criticized for over-categorizing mysticism, and particularly for placing Christian mysticism as the highest kind of mysticism. Others have attempted different categorizations of mysticism.

Despite these attempts to understand and categorize mysticism, the actual mystical belief that all religions are essentially the same is not a rational or logical argument. Rather, it is founded on what is called the *philosophia perennis.* Zaehner described this as

> That philosophy which maintains that the ultimate truths about God and the universe cannot be directly expressed in words, that these truths are necessarily everywhere and always the same, and that, therefore, the revealed religions which so obviously differ on so many major points from one another, can only be relatively true, each revelation being accommodated to the needs of the time and place in which it was made and adapted to the degree of spiritual enlightenment of its recipients . . . All are rather facets of the same

truth . . . The truth itself is that experienced by the mystics whose unity of thought and language is said to speak for itself. [5]

This *philosophia perennis* cannot then be combated by rational debate. Trying to argue in that fashion with mysticism is like trying to score a home run in a game of football; it is making what logicians call a category error, like comparing apples with pears. Mysticism does not aim to be rational, and it is no worry to it that it is not.

What then can be said about it? To begin with we need to grant the validity of these experiences. A few samples of mystical experience will be enough to convince us that the subjects of the experiences are not lying but have found something important to them. Lord Tennyson described his mystical experience in this way, recorded by William James:

> I have never had any revelations through anesthetics, but a kind of waking trance—this for lack of a better word—I have frequently had, quite up from boyhood, when I have been all alone. This has come upon me through repeating my name to myself till all at once, as it were out of the intensity of the consciousness of individuality, individuality itself seems to dissolve and fade away into boundless being, and this is not a confused state but the clearest, the surest of the sure, utterly beyond words—where death was an almost laughable impossibility—the loss of personality (if so it were) seemed no extinction, but the only true life. I am ashamed of my feeble description. Have I not said the state is utterly beyond words.[6]

A description of Islamic mysticism (Sufism) by the great Muslim scholar and mystic al-Ghazali reads:

> The mystics, after their ascent to the heaven of Reality, agree that they saw nothing in existence except God the One . . . Nothing was

---

5. R.C. Zaehner, *Mysticism Sacred and Profane* (Oxford University Press 1957), p.2.

6. W. James, *The Varieties of Religious Experience* (Longmans Green and Co. 1902), p.384.

left to them but God. They became drunk with a drunkenness in which their reason collapsed . . . However, when their drunkenness abates and the sovereignty of their reason is restored . . . they know that this was not their actual identity, but that it resembled identity as when lovers say at the height of their passion: 'I am he whom I desire and he whom I desire is I; We are two souls inhabiting one body.'[7]

The following is an account of the experience of the female Christian mystic, Julian of Norwich:

Also in this he showed me a little thing, the quantity of a hazelnut, in the palm of my hand; and it was as round as a ball. I looked upon it with the eye of my understanding, and I thought what is this. And it was answered generally in this way: it is all that is made. I marveled how it might last, for I thought it might suddenly have fallen to nothing for its smallness . . . Until I utterly become one with God, I may never have rest nor bliss that is to say, until I am so attached to him that there is nothing that is made standing between my God and me.[8]

These experiences carry a conviction, passion and note of authenticity which is compelling. However, this does not mean that the idea of the *philosophia perennis* is established. That philosophy states that mystical experience witnesses to the basic oneness of all religions. It regards the mystics as the athletes of the religious life, going further and deeper until they penetrate to the very essence of all religions. The difficulties with accepting this idea, though, are profound.

First, if we take the mystics at their word it seems that they have experienced something *beyond words*. Yet here is a large difficulty. They describe their experience as an essential oneness to reality, but how can we be sure that that is what they experienced when they them-

---

7. *Mishkat Al-Anwar* (The Niche for Lights), trans. W H T Gairdner, The Royal Asiatic Society 1924, pp. 60-61 (Revised Translation).

8. Julian of Norwich, *The Sixteen Revelations of Divine Love*. R F S Cressy 1670, ch. 5, p.11. (My own paraphrase).

selves say that what they experienced was beyond description? It seems that the *philosophia perennis* is trying to have its cake and eat it as well. If the experience is beyond description then let us leave it at that: we cannot accept an *interpretation* (which involves words and description) of that experience if interpretation is exactly what that experience transcends.

Second, precious few people seem to have had a mystical experience of the oneness of reality. Books of mystical experience tend to quote the same experiences of the same people over and over again. But there are countless thousands of devotees of different religions and most of them have never had a mystical experience. Why is this? Perhaps it is a sign of the extreme ardor and special devotion required for mystical experience. But even if that is so, it is difficult to feel secure about accepting an interpretation of the whole of the religious tradition of humanity based upon such a select few. Can they really be said to be *representative*?

Granted, then, that there are severe difficulties with accepting the *philosophia perennis* view of mystical experience we are still left with the fact of mystical experience. We have seen that this cannot be sneered at. Is there a better way of interpreting the data of mystical experience than the *philosophia perennis*? I think so.

First, the obvious similarities between mystical experiences do not necessarily mean that mystical experiences are in touch with the same reality. In fact, it may well be that the reason for the similarity of mystical experience is because mysticism is influenced by similar historical sources. The Judaeo-Christian and Islamic mystics are, it is widely acknowledged, influenced by the Greek philosophy known as "Neo-Platonism." That being so, it is not surprising that they bear similarities in style, content, and descriptive terminology. They had the same parent and bear the family likeness. The Indian mystics are in a similar fashion very reliant on each other. Their experiences, doctrines and ascetic and ecstatic practices have been shared. No wonder they appear alike. What is more, it may be that Neo-Platonism itself was influenced by Indian thought.

Second, from a scientific point of view there can be no question that as human beings we are part of the physical world. The Bible also tells us that we are made of the earth. Perhaps under certain circumstances and in certain situations we can experience this fact. Mystical experience could well be a deep consciousness of our basic biochemical unity with the world.

Third, then, it becomes clear that mysticism is not just interpreted through the mesh of different religious beliefs but is a part of those beliefs. In other words, there is not one universal mystical experience. There is certainly a Hindu mystical experience, and there is a Muslim mystical experience; there may even be a drug-induced mystical experience, but there is no universal, common mystical experience. I am not alone in this conclusion as the contemporary scholar of mysticism Stephen Katz makes the same judgment: there is no *philosophia perennis.*

It therefore follows that Christian revelation cannot be swept aside. Because the height of God's self-revelation in the incarnation makes sense, we may not think it is an irrational concept. Because Christian revelation is unique, we may not relegate it to being simply "religious" in general. We must come to terms with the actual historical revelation of God in Jesus Christ. We have seen that humanity is faced with a problem of spiritual experience that the Bible calls "sin." We have made passing reference to Jesus being the solution to sin. Now we come to see that the revelation of Jesus shows us his supremacy by proclaiming him as the savior or rescuer from sin at the cross.

13

THE CROSS SHOWS US JESUS' SUPREMACY

When Westerners think of a cross they think of a piece of jewelry or a religious artifact. When people from the Middle East think of a cross, they remember the Crusades, war and bloodshed. Both are tragic departures from reality. The cross of Jesus was something basic and barbaric. It was a crude and deadly instrument of torture, used widely in the ancient world by the Romans as judicial punishment of the most severe kind. It was certainly not a pretty sight when Jesus hung on a cross. Neither was it a symbol of might and power and empire. As Jesus breathed his last and cried out, "My God, my God, why have you forsaken me!" no one watching could have taken it for a sign of imperialism.

We live with these idols of the cross ever present in our mind. It is hard for us to divest ourselves of the overtones the word "cross" carries. And yet if we are to come to terms with its message we need somehow to picture it once more.

To begin with, we need to realize that for a cross to show anyone's supremacy is tantamount to contradiction. How can anyone reign from an electric chair? How can someone be worshiped while wearing a hangman's noose? But this seems to be almost exactly what the Bible tells us is in fact the case. Paul argues in Philippians chapter 2 that Jesus humbled himself to die and *therefore* God exalted him to the highest place. This strange emphasis upon the cross is exemplified in the throne room of heaven. There, we are told, the angels sing, "Worthy is the Lamb, who was slain, to receive power and wealth and wisdom and strength and honor and glory and praise!" (Revelation 5:12). The Lamb—that is, Jesus — is worthy of glory, power and honor *because* he was slain. Or even more strikingly, "See, the lion of the tribe of Judah . . . has triumphed . . . .Then I saw a Lamb, looking as if it had been slain, standing in the center of the throne . . ." (Revelation 5:5–6). The Lion —another metaphor for Jesus—has triumphed *because* the Lamb has been slain.

If, then, Jesus is supreme, it is without pride or self aggrandizement. This King was slain, this Lion was slaughtered like a lamb, his greatness is humble. Jesus himself identified this humility as central to his mission and calling when he said that he "did not come to be served, but to serve, and to give his life as a ransom for many" (Mark 10:45).

Accepting this as the heart of the Christian message and of the purpose of Jesus is essential if we are to embrace his supremacy. So many of us have been bruised by legalistic perceptions of religion. We have had rules and regulations shoved down our throats. And we find it very hard to hear of God without thinking of law. I cannot tell you that there is not law in God. As we shall see, rightly understood the justice of God is a precious truth. But Jesus does not come to us first asking us to be servants; he comes to us first asking us to let him serve. In fact, when Jesus encountered a woman who served him and a woman who opened her heart to him, he commended the listening of the second woman. "Martha, you are worried and upset about many things, but only one thing is needed" (Luke 10:41–2). The one thing is to trust Jesus, to open ourselves to him and to let him serve us.

This is the function of the cross. The cross is God's means of bringing people into relationship with him. The Bible gives different word pictures of the function of the cross, including judicial acquittal in a law court, freedom from slavery, appeasing wrath, and restoring friends. The picture of acquittal is conjured up by the word "justification" (Romans 5:18), freedom by "redemption" (Galatians 3:13), turning away anger by "atoning sacrifice" (1 John 4:10) and restoring friendship by "reconciliation" (2 Corinthians 5:18–19). He is our "sacrifice" (bringing to mind Old Testament animal sacrifices) for sins (Hebrews 9:26).

At different times people have stressed different aspects of the function of the cross, probably partly as a reflection of the culture of their age. Today people are most often drawn to emphasize the cross as making us friends with God. This "friendship" seems to scratch where we itch: we feel lonely and God offers to fill the void. This is a wonderful truth. But the other pictures of the cross are also wonderful truths and, rightly understood, equally relevant. We feel guilty but because of the cross we can be forgiven. We feel enslaved by unworthy desires but the cross can set us free. We feel that God is angry with us but through the cross we can find peace with him. The cross functions as salvation in its deepest and widest sense.

But not only does the cross have a *function*, it also has a *voice*. As John Stott said in his book *The Cross of Christ*, "the cross is a word as well as a work." It reveals something about God's character. And it is important that we learn to listen to the voice of the cross today. This revelation speaks a word to our land where gods are fashionable.

Kant said that it is impossible to penetrate to the essence of God. And we find in consequence that many people experiment or are interested in diverse manifestations of spirituality, without claiming absolute truth. If there are many paths up a mountain, people are content to find that the summit is unattainable or does not exist. There is joy in the journey, at least, but personally encountering the Supreme Being of the universe is untenable. The cross tells us, however, that this Being has come down. The incarnation explains that Jesus is the God-man who broke into space and time; the cross and the resurrection prove his identity. We may not be able to reach him. Kant was right in this sense: there is a barrier between God and humans. Christians do not claim to have access to God because they are cleverer or better than other people. They have not penetrated to the secrets of the universe. The secret of the universe has penetrated to them. The "mystery" (meaning something hidden or secret) has been revealed, the Bible tells us, in Jesus Christ (Colossians 1:26–7). The cross authenticates this and draws us to put our trust in this Supreme Being.

Specifically, the cross reveals two things about God. These are two matters with which many struggle, especially when it comes to the idea of Jesus' pre-eminence. The cross shows us that God is just and that God is love. Both of these are difficult things to believe in a world of pain and hardship. But each is displayed at the cross in a way that draws out our faith in Jesus' supremacy.

Because we have all suffered, we find it hard to believe God is just. It may be that none is completely innocent but many people seem to suffer beyond their just deserts. When we suffer we feel aggrieved at God. "Why did he let his happen?" we ask. We may find it hard to believe that there is a God at all, at least a just or good God. In my work I have the privilege of listening to people's personal problems. Sometimes I come away from a day of preaching and pastoring amazed at the mundane horror of life. This person has told me about a terrible illness that plagues them. That person has described their abusive husband. How can God be good when he lets these things happen?

There is no simplistic "answer" to this question. We all suffer, and we all puzzle about it. But a Christian can respond by pointing to the cross. At the cross God himself suffered in some profound way. And at the cross God shows us that he will not let evil go unpunished. He will not sit on his hands and let the world go blithely to the dogs. He will act—he has acted. And it cost Jesus his life.

The Bible plumbs the depths of this profundity when it says in a famous passage.

> God prepared him [Jesus] as a sacrifice of atonement, through faith in his blood. He did this to demonstrate his justice, because in his forbearance he had left the sins committed beforehand unpun- ished—he did it to demonstrate his justice at the present time, so as to be just and the one who justifies those who have faith in Jesus. (Romans 3:25–6).

God has demonstrated his justice: the passage emphasizes this by repeating the fact. He has definitely and finally declared that he is good.

I know that this does not resolve every difficulty with accepting the supremacy of God. We still hurt at times. We will have questions about God's rule in a suffering world. But the cross does not have only a message of justice; it also has a message of love. In another famous passage the Bible tells us: "But God demonstrates his own love for us in this: While we were still sinners, Christ died for us" (Romans 5:8).

In other words, the cross speaks of love as well as of justice. The cross says, "This is the extent to which God is prepared to go to sort our lives out." It tells us that God did not wait for us to sort ourselves out. To think that he does is the grand mistake of all false religion. In authentic spirituality God is always the initiator. He does not wait for us to be holy before he loves us. He died for us while we were bad and, even though we are frail and broken and all too human, he loves us. He loves, period. There is no "because" in God's love. He loves us. Why? He is love.

For many people this is a message that is hard to internalize because their experience of love has not been of this kind. Their parents brought them up on a diet of "conditional love." In all sorts of subtle ways the message sent was that they were loved when they were good. Or they have been in relationships that have broken up when the other person was bored or annoyed with them. The message sent is that you are loved when you are worth loving. The cross runs counter to all this conditional love. It is unconditional love. We need to look at the cross, where it is displayed. As John says in his first letter, "This is love: not that we loved God, but that he loved us" (1 John 4:10). God has set a sign in history which says, "This is how much I love you."

In our land where gods are fashionable the message of the cross speaks with power. The cross has always been the key to unlock the door to people's hearts. Historical debates about the cross illustrate the importance of rediscovering its message for each generation. In the early church a discussion arose about whether the cross actually did something to save us or whether it acted merely as an example to encourage us to save ourselves. At the Reformation, in the sixteenth century, the Western church split over the function of the cross when a controversy brewed over the extent of the cross's work. More recently in the twentieth century a dispute similar to that in the early church occurred, about whether Jesus' death was primarily an example or a sacrifice. What is the debate now? Today, we need to learn to rely on the cross for our spiritual experience and for our presentation of Christianity. The land where gods are fashionable tempts us to say that the cross is no longer relevant. But actually the cross is the source of spiritual power, the center of the Christian message, the display of the antidote to this land: the supremacy of Jesus.

In practical terms Jesus attracts an extraordinary diversity of followers. Once in my student days I was hitch-hiking from Scotland to England and was stranded outside Glasgow. I waited and waited, watching vehicles scream past me ignoring my thumb. At last a truck stopped—and the driver agreed to take me all the way down to London. We struck up a conversation and for some reason or other we began to talk about God. As we talked, I discovered some surprising things about this trucker. He had not always been a truck driver but earlier in his life was the lead singer of a fairly well-known rock group. It turned out that he was longing to hear about God and how to get into a relationship with him.

On the road to Jesus there are truck drivers and hitch-hikers, rockers and students, singers and preachers. There is no aspect of the universe, no corner of the globe, no type of person, no cultural anomaly over which Jesus does not have the supremacy.

SECTION 4

THE EXPERIENCE OF THE SPIRIT

. . . live by the Spirit . . .
Galatians 5:16

14

IT'S ABOUT GODLINESS

Authentic spiritual experience is not produced by godliness. We are not made spiritual by trying to be holy. Real spirituality is given not earned, by faith and not by works. It starts with what God has done for us in Jesus and not with what we do for him. However, godliness *is* a product of authentic spiritual experience. Confusing these two things (what produces spiritual experience and what is produced by spiritual experience) is common. It is also disastrous. Technically speaking, to say that being holy produces spiritual experience is to advocate "legalism." It is to say that obeying God is what grants us his pleasure, a sense of his presence. On the other hand, to deny that authentic spiritual experience must produce holiness is what is known as "antinomianism." It denies that obedience to God necessarily results from authentic spirituality.

As we come to consider the experience of the Spirit we need to keep both these pitfalls in mind. In this section we are asking the question "How can we tell what is a real experience of God and what is not?" To answer that correctly means steering a middle path between legalism and antinomianism.

According to an ancient Greek myth, there is a place where seafarers must beware the rocks of Scylla on the one hand and Charybdis on the other. Sailing too close to either danger would be fatal to a ship. Similarly, we need to stay clear of both the dangers mentioned above, legalism and antinomianism.

To do so is far from easy. Spiritual experience means experience of God. Testing the reality and truth of our spiritual experience means examining a divine encounter. Say you have managed to carve out for yourself one of those rare quiet moments. You are away from your daily responsibilities and distractions, the children are in bed and the TV is off. For me those are times when I begin to reflect. I think about my life, where I am going; I feel again some of the past pains and scars of my own personal history. What you think and feel in those moments is private to you. But I can guarantee that one element of that reflection is common to everyone. Our life seems terribly complex. Great men and women can simplify the very complex, but only children think that things are really simple. When we "get in touch with ourselves" we find that this "self" is an amazingly complex being. Now if we experience ourselves like that, what can it possibly be like to experience God? If, I, small and finite, am that complex to experience, then experience of God must be infinitely more complex.

We should not be surprised, then, at the confusion there is concerning spiritual experience. We are dealing with something difficult. What we need is to return to that place where we can hear God speak to us through the confusion. Our emotions and psychologies are mazes of wrong turns; the Bible is as straight as an arrow and as sharp as a double-edged sword.

15

TESTING SPIRITUALITY: ANY OLD GOD WILL *NOT* DO

In the third land of our present world there is confusion. Some are confident that their particular mode of spirituality is the genuine one. Others vehemently deny that it is and propose an alternative pattern of spiritual experience. At this point two temptations face us. One is the "baby-and-bath-water" fallacy. Here we discard all spirituality because the arguments about it seem to suggest that we cannot be certain about it. The confusion turns us off God or at least radical dealings with God and we end up throwing out God with the confusion, the baby with the bath water. The other temptation is the "hook-line-and-sinker" mistake. We swallow all claims to spiritual experience, unwilling or unable to countenance the idea that some may be false. In either case, we need to realize that spirituality can be tested.

This is not to be judgmental. When the Bible tells us not to judge it means that we should not presume to know *who* will be saved. It does not mean that we should not know *how* we shall be saved. After all, it is mainly written to make sure we do know how we can be saved. Neither is testing spirituality doing what the Bible calls "putting God to the test." When the Bible tells us not to do this it does not intend us to accept without question every person who claims to speak for God. It means that we should not treat God as a plaything, someone we can command at our whim, like a genie in a lamp that does its master's bidding. God is our master; we are not his. But we can, and indeed should, test spirituality. All that glitters is not gold and all that seems spiritual is not authentic.

Testing spirituality is a vital task because while ours is a time of spiritual openness not seen for many years, it is also a time of danger. Suggesting that God is dead is a spiritual blind spot, but is equally blind to suggest that any old god will do. A lie is a lie, and it does not much matter whether we believe that any spirituality is as good as any other or that there is no spirituality—both are wrong. What's more, new lies can be harder to nail than old ones: they catch you unaware. The devil you know is sometimes better than the devil you do not know. The challenge in the twenty-first century will be to catch this new devil by the tail; that is, in biblical terms, to "test the spirits."

The question, then, we must answer is this: What are the criteria we are to use to test whether something is a true experience of God's presence?

WHAT THE BIBLE SAYS ABOUT SPIRITUALITY

The Bible is clearly the first and last port of call. But, having said that, the answer to our question is not an open-and-shut case. Certainly, it needs to be said that as far as the Bible is concerned, there really is only one source of true spirituality. Biblical spiritual experience comes through faith in Christ realized in the present by the work of the Holy Spirit. As far as the Scriptures are concerned, any other kind of spirit is evil. But once Christians have accepted the gospel, they find many patterns of spirituality claimed as biblical, some reassuringly familiar, others unnervingly bizarre. At this point we get confused and need to see four things said about spirituality in the Bible.

1. Not everything. . . .

The Bible does not teach us everything, but says very little about many subjects. It says nothing about molecular biology, the history of the Weimar Republic, or the atmospheric conditions of Mars. Of course, it does say a lot about how we can approach science, history and astronomy, but within these fields God has left some things for us to discover, using the creativity he has endowed us with. And it is the same with the way we react to spiritual forces; the Bible does not say everything there is to know. Some of it is basic psychology. We are emotional beings. If God touches me powerfully in some way, I am extremely likely to react emotionally. It would be strange if I did not! For the God of the whole universe to communicate with me and for me not to feel anything seems almost impossible. However, because we are emotional beings, to have an emotional reaction similar to one I would expect to have if God did speak to me, does not necessarily mean that he *has* spoken. After all, you can feel the same kind of emotions at any rock concert.

2. But principles . . .

However, rather than give us a description of every possible spiritual experience, or a prescription of allowed spiritual experiences, the Bible gives us principles by which to test the two sorts of spiritual experiences: principles concerning "roots" and principles concerning the "fruits." The picture is Christ's who said, "Likewise every good tree bears good fruit, but a bad tree bears bad fruit . . . Thus by their fruit you will recognize them" (Matthew 7:17–20).

3. About roots . . .

The heart, not the head, is the center of the spiritual experience most commonly described in the Bible. This is the wellspring of spiritual life (Proverbs 4:23), hardened by sin, but softened by the Holy Spirit (Ezekiel 36:26), the place in which the roots of true spirituality grow. Some tend to think that the head is where true knowledge is found. The heart seems altogether unreliable; it flutters into cheap romances and falls out of love too.

But what the Bible means by "heart" is not this. It uses the word to mean not merely emotions but the whole disposition of a person, including emotion, reason and will. In Bible terms, what you have a heart for is what your heart is set upon; it is what you are about, what you want, what you love. You might say that the "heart" is the feeling of our heads and the thinking of our hearts. It is a warm, intuitive knowledge rather than cold rational logic.

True spirituality needs to be rooted in the heart. A seventeenth-century group of Christians called the Puritans used to express it by saying that "notional" knowledge was not enough; it was necessary to have "experimental" knowledge as well. In other words, if you have real spirituality you cannot just think about God, you have to feel him too, and vice versa. We need to recover this intuition. For years Christians had fought so hard on the "thinking" front that when someone began to think about God, we were tempted to call them a Christian. Today, that is a dangerous assumption; with the gods back on the agenda, there may be many spiritualities that stem from some vague "notional" belief that have no "experimental" knowledge of God at all.

4. And fruits . . .

However, we do not have spiritual X-ray vision. Only God can see the heart (Psalm 44:21; Proverbs 17:3; 21:2). The way he tells us to test heart spirituality is by its "fruits," by what spirituality produces. But the great mistake is to conclude that if something produces religious experiences then it must be of God. It is not so easy: fruits test the roots, the heart. Heart knowledge cannot be any kind of spiritual knowledge but a true knowledge of God. Therefore, the fruits envisaged point to a specific work of grace in the heart. Not all fruits are true fruits. One person may seem loving and yet inwardly selfish (you scratch my back and I'll scratch yours); another may look peaceful and yet be merely lazy (God is in control so I'll do nothing); another may seem to be a person full of the Spirit but in reality be full of self.

The Bible clearly defines the kind of fruit to look for. The most exhaustive list of the fruits of the Spirit is given in Galatians 5:22–3. This passage is in many ways a description of Christ, of the way in which the Spirit intends to make us Christ-like. But it does not pick out the most significant of these signs of spirituality—it is a flat description. The mountain-top, we know from 1 Corinthians 13:13, is the first on the list, which is love. This love produces action, for it is love that obeys Christ (John 14:21). And it is the action that comes from love which Christ picks out as the pre-eminent sign of true spirituality in Matthew 25:40, when he gives his final assessment of spirituality on Judgment Day: "I tell you the truth, whatever you did for one of the least of these brothers of mine, you did for me." Love is not mentioned in this verse, but the fruit of it is. The greatest sign of true spirituality is the love for Christ, which creates love for people, overflowing into practical Christian activity. What the people described in Matthew 25 *did* evidence their fate on Judgment Day, not because they were saved by such works, but because the works were a sign of their heart love for Christ, of their true faith in Christ. True spirituality produces the activity that is generated by Christian love. This is very different from saying that works produces true spirituality; they do not. True spirituality produces works. Testing spirituality correctly means steering an equal distance from the rocks of legalism on the one hand and antinomianism on the other.

In other words, any old god will not do. Only true spirituality; obedience to the Lord Jesus Christ, will produce right action.

If only true spirituality will do, we need to think carefully about its nature and be sure we are practicing it. So let us look at a case study which applies the biblical guidelines for testing and experiencing the presence of God.

16

BIBLICAL MODELS OF SPIRITUALITY

Being able to test a spiritual experience is not the same as having one. Many of us are good critics but bad playwrights. But in the Christian life one cannot stay in the stands for long; we have to get into the game to really know it. The Bible gives us models of spirituality to help us investigate spiritual experience from the inside. These models are not intended to advance our theoretical knowledge alone. They are designed to provide insight, awareness and a route to knowing the presence of God in our daily lives.

The path to the presence of God is to dig deep into the mines of the Christian gospel. This gospel is the message of Jesus Christ, to "Repent and believe the good news" (Mark 1:14). Sometimes we think that the answer to our spiritual malaise must be novel or complex. We think that because our problems with God are difficult, the solution to those problems must be difficult as well. There is a sense in which that intuition is correct. Jesus said that the road to life was narrow and few find it. But there is also a sense in which it is incorrect. Sometimes the answers to the most intransigent problems are simple. This is often the case in the spiritual life. The difficulties come with accepting the answer, not with the complexity of the answer itself.

An Old Testament story of a military leader illustrates the difficulty of simplicity in the spiritual life. He had been diagnosed with a rare skin disease. Everything had been tried to cure him, but nothing worked. Finally, in desperation, he visited a prophet. We can imagine the embarrassment this was to a no-nonsense general, made worse by the fact that the prophet was an enemy of the nation the military leader represented. Insult was added to injury when, after a long arduous journey, the prophet did not even deign to see the general. Instead, a messenger appeared and told him to wash seven times. Wash? He could have washed at home. What made this little stream better than the great river in his country?

The general did wash, however, and was healed. The point of the story is not that washing seven times cures skin disease. It tells us that simple solutions are difficult. They require humility to accept. Experiencing genuine spirituality requires the humility simply to trust the gospel.

God reveals the gospel through his word, Jesus Christ and the Holy Spirit. These are three biblical models of spirituality. By them we may increase our trust in the gospel and so also our experience of spirituality.

THE WORD

Psalm 119 is the longest psalm in the Bible. Its length has cowed commentators. One of the most able expositors of the Psalms was initially bewildered by it. "Other Psalms," wrote Charles Spurgeon, "have been mere lakes, but this is the main ocean." Its great extent has also been put to expedient use. Making the most of the old custom that a condemned criminal could ask for a psalm to be sung before execution, George Whishart asked for Psalm 119. Two-thirds of the way through reciting the psalm he received a timely pardon!

But despite that psalm's size, we can readily pinpoint three of its aspects that unearth its message about spirituality.

First, the psalm's theme is the Word of God. Every verse of the 176 verses (bar verse 122) has a reference to God's Word. It uses various synonyms for this word. Second, its poetic structure is known to be "acrostic" or alphabetic. Every stanza begins with a different letter of the Hebrew alphabet, and each verse repeats the letter of the stanza. And third, the psalm is recognized to strike a constant note of praise, even in the midst of hardship.

This provides us with three facts about the psalm. Its content is the word, its structure is alphabetic, and its style is worship. We have, then, the "A–Z of word praise." The psalm is an exhaustive acclamation of the importance of the Word of God.

Our analysis of the psalm means that authentic spirituality should be written with the language of this word alphabet. The Word of God should not make us "wordy" or "bookish." It should give us knowledge of the presence of God in all depth and breadth of his whole A–Z of spiritual experience.

The Word should give us deep emotional engagement with God. Psalm 119 describes a person who feels profoundly about the Word. "I open my mouth and pant, longing for your commands" (v. 131), the writer of the psalm says in one place. He tells us that "Streams of tears flow from my eyes, for your law is not obeyed" (v.136). He obeys God's commands because "I love them greatly" (v.167).

We should rely on the Word even when people scoff at us. The psalmist is surrounded by those who "have forsaken the law" and by those who are "double-minded" (v.113), who are two-faced in their allegiance. These people "dig pitfalls" (v.85) for him. They have "smeared" him (v.69). But even if "I constantly take my life in my hands" (v. 109) and "they almost wiped me from the earth" (v. 87), he will not forget the law.

And we can obey the Word not in our own power but in God's. This psalm is not moralizing; a deep reliance upon the Lord permeates throughout it. The psalmist knows he needs to be saved to obey the law, not obey the law to be saved: "I call out to you; save me and I will keep your statues" (v. 146). He is humble enough to say, "I have strayed like a lost sheep. Seek your servant, for I have not forgotten your commandments" (v. 176).

JESUS CHRIST

In the Bible all the lines of authentic spirituality converge in Jesus. There are four areas of this *Christian* spirituality we could outline.

1. Christian spirituality exalts the honor of Jesus. We have seen that the Word of God occupies a central place in authentic spirituality. But the Word made flesh is Jesus: he is the ultimate self-revelation of God (John 1:14). He is the final Word (Hebrews 1:2). He is the risen Lord of the universe (Colossians 1:18), the one before whom one day every knee shall bow (Philippians 2:10). As such he requires total allegiance and complete obedience.

2. Christian spirituality follows the example of Jesus. Paul tells us that our attitude should be the same as that of Christ Jesus (Philippians 2:5). Authentic spirituality is not superficial, but orientates our whole mind pattern toward Jesus. We too should be humble. We too should be servants. We too should be able to say, "God's will be done," even at our most extreme hour of trial.

3. Christian spirituality learns from the teaching of Jesus. Those who listened to Jesus remarked that he taught "with authority" (Mark 1:27). His instruction was not derived from others but was peppered with the divine "I tell you" (Matthew 5:21-2, 27-8, 31-2, etc.). Christian spirituality recognizes his teaching as supremely authoritative.

4. Christian spirituality focuses on the death and resurrection of Jesus. The cross was Jesus' goal. Jesus said time and again that he "must" die, that he "must" go to Jerusalem where he would be crucified and rise again from the dead. He said that he came into the world "to give his life as a ransom for many" (Mark 10:45). Jesus' purpose is the focal point of Christian spirituality.

5. Christian spirituality views world history and personal experience in the light of Jesus. Given that Christian spirituality exalts Jesus, follows Jesus, listens to Jesus and has Jesus' death and resurrection at its center of devotion, our worldview and sense of place in history is defined by Jesus as well. For us, life is not meandering in a constant cycle, but rather the world has come from somewhere and is going somewhere (or to someone). Life is about Jesus Christ, and all of life and existence finds its meaning in him.

This last is worthy of emphasis. It is easy to make emotive appeals to be like Jesus in every respect without asking what that signifies. Jesus had no home, was crucified, and performed miracles. Does that mean that all *real* disciples of Jesus will do the same? Christians believe that we should all be like Jesus. But they do not believe that we should all be savior of the world. Between those two statements lies a spiritual minefield. The sixteenth century church leader Martin Luther once came across old people playing hoops in the streets in supposed obedience to Christ's command to "become as little children."

But the focus of Christian spirituality is on the death and resurrection of Jesus. "Preaching Jesus" means proclaiming forgiveness of sins through faith in the cross. Worshiping Jesus is having hearts, lips, and lives shaped by gratitude for his death. Being like little children does not mean being stuck in permanent psychological infancy, but acknowledging dependency upon the death of Jesus for our salvation. The few people during Jesus' lifetime who realized that his goal was to die are highlighted for special praise in the New Testament accounts. A woman who anointed his body to prepare it for death was commended. Jesus said that wherever the gospel was preached her action would be remembered. She was applauded because her action illustrated that death was Jesus' purpose.

Each generation needs to rediscover Jesus. We surround his challenging words with religious ritual. We soft-pedal Jesus until being like him is very close to being like us. We assume that our way is right, our method is best, and that our will should be done. But the Jesus of the Bible shakes our traditions.

THE HOLY SPIRIT

1. The nature of the Holy Spirit

The Holy Spirit is not a "force," but a person. We should not think of the Spirit as an "it," an impersonal power, but as a "he." He has a character, a personality; he is *someone* not *something*. The Holy Spirit is God. Jesus tells his disciples to baptize people not just in the name of the Son or just in the name of the Father, but in the name of the Father, Son and Holy Spirit (Matthew 28:19). We can appreciate the significance of this by replacing the Spirit with an alternative "name." Jesus would not have told his disciples to baptize people in the name of the Father, Son, and the archangel Gabriel. The last words of Jesus in Matthew's Gospel set apart the Holy Spirit as co-equal God. It is not surprising, then, that Paul assumes the divinity of the Holy Spirit, signing off his letters with a "blessing" from God: "May the grace of the Lord Jesus Christ, and the love of God, and the fellowship of the Holy Spirit be with you all" (2 Corinthians 13:14). Or that Peter rebukes two early church members for having lied to the Holy Spirit because they "have not lied to men but to God" (Acts 5:3–4).

The divinity of the Holy Spirit is part of the Christian teaching known as the "Trinity." In consequence, before proceeding we need to make sure that we are clear about this concept and its coherence.

In concept the Trinity is not different *modes* or departments of God, called the Father, Son and Holy Spirit, but a belief that all are *equally* God. The Trinity is not an expression of the different roles of God but is his core nature. The Christian teaching of the Trinity is that God is three persons and that each person is fully God and that God is one.

Understandably, people have found the Trinity difficult to swallow, but its coherence can be defended as reliable truth. To do so we need to be confident and humble. We should be confident because the charge that the Trinity is incoherent or irrational is unfounded. It may be true that one plus one plus one is three, but it does not follow that Christians really believe in three Gods. After all, one times one times one is one. But we are not dealing with math here; we are dealing with the infinite God, and we need also to be humble. It is an embarrassment only to human pride that there is an element of mystery to the Trinity; the essence of God will be above the grasp of our minds. However, if God is our creator we may humbly expect there to be a Trinitarian imprint reflected in the natural world. And, indeed, there is a complexity yet unity to existence. Light, for instance, is made up of particles *and* waves. At a "one plus one plus one" level this does not make sense. Something cannot be both a particle and a wave. But science has discovered that light is waves and particles. Reality is complex, as is God.

2. The empowering presence of the Holy Spirit

The theologian Wayne Grudem defines the Holy Spirit's role as to "make known the presence of God in the world, and specifically the church." The presence of the Spirit distinguishes the Christian church and is the privilege of all who put their trust in Jesus (Acts 2:16–21; Romans 8:9–11). The power of the Holy Spirit enables Christians to live as children of God (Galatians 4:6–7; Romans 8:14–16). Sadly, people have sometimes abused talk of the presence or the power of the Spirit in manipulative ways. Power corrupts. But the Holy Spirit is incorruptible, even though he does have absolute power. His presence is always Christ-like not cult-like.

The influence of the Spirit's presence is both powerfully proclaimed and carefully described in chapter 5 of Paul's letter to the Galatians. Paul is aware of two dangers. He warns the Galatians against "moralism" or "legalism," the idea that you can get into God's good books by human moral effort and religious ritual. And he warns against immorality or "license," the idea that sin and evil do not matter to God. Christians are not slaves to religious rules but neither are they slaves to immoral practices. The Holy Spirit is neither a "legalistic" nor an "antinomian" spirit. His presence empowers us to live as Jesus wants. Jesus has set Christians free and they are to stay free (v. 1) but they are to use this freedom to live as Jesus intended, which is a life of love (vv. 13–14).

Paul tells us that we are to "live by the Spirit" (v.16), "be led by the Spirit" (v.18), and "keep in step with the Spirit" (v.25). These phrases mean that we need consciously and purposefully to rely on the Spirit for our living, guiding, and walking. This deliberate reliance upon the Spirit is brought out by the structure of the passage. It is constructed in a kind of literary tension. A sort of comparison or distinction runs from the top to the bottom, producing tension, like a stress fracture on a wall that runs from the ceiling to the floor. The tension is between the sinful nature and the Spirit: we are either living by the Spirit or gratifying the sinful nature.

Paul portrays this tension by comparing the works of the sinful nature with the fruit of the Spirit. Christians live in the tension of both sinful nature and the Holy Spirit tugging against each other. The acts of the sinful nature are a jarring disunity ("acts" in the plural); the fruit of the Spirit is a single united expression of a God of love ("fruit" in the singular). The acts of the sinful nature tail off into constant painful and dull repetition ("and the like", v.21); the fruit of the Spirit climaxes in spiritual freedom ("Against such things there is no law", v.23). The sinful nature is the remainder of a taste for sin that dogs the footsteps of the most holy person ("you do not do what you want", v.17); the fruit of the Spirit is a dynamic of spiritual growth that is given by God (we "live" by the Spirit, v.16; we are "led" by the Spirit, v. 18; we have the "fruit" of the Spirit, v.22).

Our human nature exerts a constant gravitational pull towards self-ishness and wrongdoing. God's Spirit releases people to be full of love for God and others. Reading this passage is intended to make us cry out in need of the empowering presence of the Spirit.

But needing the Spirit requires practice. I am a very occasional golfer. By occasional I mean that I have played the game not more than a dozen times in my life and only once in the last two years. I am not even sure I know what a handicap is. The strange thing about golf for me, though, is that practicing seems to do me no good whatsoever. If I just wander up to the tee and give the annoyingly little white thing a good whack, then as likely as not it will go soaring off at least roughly in the right direction. If, on the other hand, I think about what I am meant to be doing beforehand, if I have a couple of practice swings like they do on the TV, I am doomed. Anyone within 20 yards of me—forwards, backwards, or sideways—had better beware!

By saying that we need to put into practice this hunger for the Spirit, I do not mean the equivalent of doing a couple of warm-up golf swings. In the English language the word "practice" is ambivalent: it either means preparing yourself for what you have to do (doing "practice papers" for exams for instance) or it means actually doing what you have to do (putting it into practice). It is in this latter sense that I mean "practice." The Galatians 5 passage encourages us to put needing the Spirit into practice.

Here are some suggestions about how to do this:

1. *Acknowledge your total reliance upon the Spirit.* That may sound a little nebulous but it is important to cultivate an attitude of needing the Spirit first. Think on Christ's words "apart from me you can do nothing" (John 15:5), or on what Paul says in Galatians chapter 5, "live by the Spirit." We want to foster the attitude not of gritting our teeth and being stoical but of relying totally upon the spiritual desires the Spirit stirs up within us.

2. *Ask God for the Spirit.* Jesus promised that our heavenly Father would give the Spirit to all who ask him (Luke 11:13). Paul tells us that since we live by the Spirit we are to keep in step with the Spirit, to progress with the Spirit (Galatians 5:25). You could pray with Paul in another place for the main fruit of the Spirit, "May the Lord make your love increase and overflow for each other and for everyone else, just as ours does for you" (1 Thessalonians 3:12).

3. *Don't allow for a wedge to be driven between Word and Spirit.* God's Spirit is connected to God's Word as breath is to speech. He who has the Spirit will be he who listens to the Word and follows its teaching, for what it is teaching is what the Holy Spirit is saying. "The sword of the Spirit, which is the Word of God" (Ephesians 6:17).

4. *Believe that the Spirit has power to vanquish your sins and your bad habits.* Trust his promises, for instance that "sin shall not be your master, because you are not under law, but under grace" Romans 6:14), or as Paul writes in Galatians chapter 5 that you "have crucified the sinful nature with its passions and desires" (v.24). It may be that a particular sin or sinful habit is solved overnight, but it is unlikely to be solved so quickly. Do not put conditions on when God must do something.

5. *Do that which the Spirit stirs up in you to do.* Relying on the Spirit, act. We walk, not sit in the Spirit; we work, not wallow in the Spirit; we fight, not flop in the Spirit. Effort is required, but the desire is the Spirit's. It is a hand-in-glove scenario: we work in God's power, but we do work. The amazing thing is that this can give us incredible confidence. Even when we are weak we can be confident because he says, "My grace is sufficient for you, for my power is made perfect in weakness" (2 Corinthians 12:9).

Experiencing real spirituality

All three elements—the Word, Jesus Christ, and the Holy Spirit—are essential for the formation of authentic spirituality. We need to treasure the Word of God. The Bible warns us against supplanting God's Word with human words:

> "Let the prophet who has a dream tell his dream, but let the one who has my word speak it faithfully. For what has straw to do with grain?" declares the Lord. "Is not my word like fire?" declares the

Lord, "and like a hammer that breaks a rock in pieces?" (Jeremiah 23:28–9).

But we also need to prioritize the message of Jesus Christ. When Jesus was revealed before James, Peter and John in his majesty, he was seen walking with the representatives of biblical law and true prophecy, with Moses and Elijah. But it was to Jesus that they were told to pay prior attention: "This is my Son, whom I love. Listen to him!" (Mark 9:2–7; see also 2 Peter 1:16–18). And we shall not be either treasuring the Word or listening to Jesus unless we do so in conscious and confident reliance upon the Holy Spirit. At Sunday school I was taught a sword drill which enforced the need for balance in this respect. "Sheath swords!" we were told, and we placed our Bibles under our arms. "Draw swords!" and we held our Bibles aloft in one hand. And then together we recited ""The sword of the Spirit is the word of God" (Ephesians 6:17). As one of Britain's greatest theologians, John Owen said, "He that would utterly separate the Spirit from the word had as good burn his Bible."

This is Christian spirituality. It is not a human spirituality but a "heavenly" one, a spirituality that honors God's word, God's Son, and God's Spirit. It cannot be manufactured or produced but depends for its power and presence upon the work and word of God himself.

For instance, my first taste of the power of the presence of God came when I was 13. I was at boarding school, gradually learning how to survive in a tough environment. There was a Christian Union at the school, but it only had about three members. It was known as the "School Christian Union Meeting" and disparagingly called SCUM for short. One week everything changed. About 100 pupils in a school of 450 made professions of faith in Christ in response to straightforward explanations of the Christian message. The CU membership leaped from 3 to 103. Many things had preceded that week, including prayer, and the witness of concerned Christian teachers. But in the end it was God who took the initiative and we who experienced his empowering presence.

To experience God we need to be willing to know his presence. Many of our attempts at being spiritual can come a little too close to what Mark Twain once said, "In our country we have those three unspeakably precious things: freedom of speech, freedom of conscience, and the prudence never to practice either of them." There are dangers of course, but we must not be like the person who resolved never to go near water until he had learned to swim! We need to take the first step to walk in authentic spirituality.

Walking is a balancing act. When we have grown up we forget how hard it is to put one foot in front of the other, but watching a baby trying to walk reminds us of when we were a "toddler." Experiencing real spirituality is like walking, the metaphor Paul uses in Galatians chapter 5. It is hard to balance the elements of the Word, Jesus, and the Holy Spirit. And then when we have learned to do so, we come across more difficult terrain that demands mature skill to keep our footing. The temptation is to leave the straight and narrow and develop a bias or tilt to one side or another.

Our family used to go walking in the Lake District. In that region there is a path that runs between two adjacent peaks. The path is so narrow that it is called Striding Edge—you can with one stride, one large step, cross from one edge to the other. On both sides there are yawning chasms. To cross that path you have to walk on the edge. Experiencing authentic spirituality is a bit like walking on Striding Edge: there are precipices on either side, and the road to life is narrow.

17

JONATHAN EDWARDS WHAT IS SPIRITUAL EXPERIENCE LIKE?

Edwards tested spirituality by its fruits. This does not mean that he was not interested in the roots of spiritual experience. Or that he believed the end justifies the means in theology and ministry. Rather, he established intricate and detailed "signs" by which to validate the source of authentic spiritual experience. He attempted to avoid two common errors of spirituality that we also need to be careful to avoid today.

These errors emerged against the background of international religious revival. Given the secular force of the Enlightenment, that there was a revival at all is initially surprising. But, partly in reaction to Enlightenment rationalism and partly as a result of the Enlightenment's newly found confidence, revival burst onto the scene in the eighteenth century. This revival is known either as "The Great Awakening" or as "The Evangelical Revival." It spanned America, Britain and parts of mainland Europe. Its best-known leaders were John Wesley, Charles Wesley (the great hymn writer), George Whitefield and Jonathan Edwards.

The revival was massively successful. But it also had its problems, as revivals do. In this case, some of the supporters of the revival became rather overzealous and brought disrepute to the movement. Later "revivalists" have copied their wild antics and sentimental ways. But the Great Awakening of Whitefield, Wesley, and Edwards was a different affair. Nevertheless, ever since it has been tarred with the same brush as the fanatics. In addition to fanaticism, the revival was also misunderstood and vigorously opposed by the institutional church of the time. Wesley and Whitefield had tremendous trouble with some of the Church of England authorities; and Edwards' arch-enemy was a leading figure among the Congregationalist churches of New England. Ironically, most Protestant institutions are now happy to claim the revival as their own.

In this maelstrom of activity and growth, errors emerged. Those who have studied the history of the church have sometimes concluded that when the church grows everything grows. When people are open to spiritual things they are also ripe for plucking by religious charlatans. Cancer is growth too, and there were two kinds of spiritual cancer that Edwards spoke against and we need to beware of today.

1. The error of deism

The first cancerous error is called "deism." Deism is a belief in a God who is distant from us. He is transcendent but not immanent. He started the ball of creation and then let it run by itself. He is not active in the world but is remote. The discoveries of science in the Enlightenment period encouraged this view of God. The more of the natural world that could be explained scientifically the less room some found to believe in God's present activity in the universe.

Often the only religion deists regarded as genuine was characterized by mental assent or rationalistic belief. Because they thought God was distant from this world they were suspicious of claims of emotional or personal engagement with him.

Deism was influential beyond the confines of those who are usually classed as deists in the history books. It reflected a contemporary and common tendency towards rationalistic religion. For instance Charles Chauncy, a renowned Boston minister in the eighteenth century, was influenced by a deistic approach to religion. His principle of spiritual experience was this: "The plain truth is that an enlightened mind, not raised affections, ought always to be the guide of those who call themselves men." Or as he also wrote, "Satan works upon the reason by the passion, the Spirit upon the passion by the reason."[9]

2. The error of "enthusiasm"

The other error was "enthusiasm." This word literally means "God within," and in the eighteenth century it was used in that sense. It indicated a belief in the direct operations of God in a person's life. In contrast to deism, enthusiasm emphasized not the distance of God but the presence or immanence of God. He was active in the world, here and now.

Enthusiasts' concept of spiritual experience was characterized by what were called "direct impressions." This meant information given or impressed upon the mind directly by God. James Davenport is a good example of this attitude. He was much given to "direct impressions." Once he made a public bonfire of books because he believed God had told him to burn them. At various times he felt divinely commissioned to declare who was and who was not a Christian. He was no fool—he was a successful leader, the son of a reputed theologian. However, in the end the ruling religious community decided that he was temporarily insane and was forced to declare: "Davenport is under the influence of enthusiastical impressions and impulses and thereby disturbed in the rational faculties of the mind."[9]

EDWARDS' RESPONSE: "SENSE" AND "SIGNS"

In response to these two errors of deism and enthusiasm Edwards proposed "sense" and "signs." He did this to set out the true nature of spiritual experience and provide a way to evaluate it. Edwards was

---

9. Charles Chauncy, *Seasonable Thoughts on the State of Religion in New England*

avoiding the dangers of legalism on the one hand and antinomianism on the other.

By "sense" Edwards intended to distinguish spiritual experience from deism and enthusiasm. He did not believe that God normally gave "direct impressions." But neither did he believe that religion should be boiled down to reason. He was sure that we can have a supernatural and personal encounter with the living God. But he was equally sure that it was important to distinguish this encounter from an imaginary one. We can depict things in our minds, we can have "impressions" internally, and some people even hear voices. But God's work is not like this. It is not fanaticism; it is not "enthusiasm." Instead, it is a sense of God.

A sense of God means "inclination toward God." It was an appreciation of who God is. For Edwards, spiritual experience primarily consisted in a "sense of the supreme beauty" of God. Edwards explained this further by asking what the difference will be between Christian and non-Christian knowledge of God on the Day of Judgment. Both will know who he is and what he is like. According to Edwards, non-Christians will know everything about God that Christians do; the only difference is that non-Christians will not like what they know.

If the source of spiritual experience is this "sense," it follows that both enthusiasm and deism made substantial errors. In a way the errors were two sides of the same coin. They each thought spiritual experience was immediate or direct. Deism just rejected this, while enthusiasm embraced it. But the Bible makes it clear that after Moses no other prophet has seen God "face to face" (Deuteronomy 34:10). We experience God through our engagement with Jesus, in the Bible and in our hearts by his Spirit. Through these means we sense the beauty of the divine being.

Edwards also responded to the errors by constructing a system of "signs," listing these in different places in his writings, and expressing them in various forms. These signs are stringent tests of spirituality. Everything about Edwards was precise, and these signs are precision *par excellence*. They should not be allowed to make us feel guilty.

Rather, they were intended to give security by discerning erroneous claims to spirituality.

The following is a sample of the signs that Edwards used:

1. True spiritual experience is shown by spiritual character, not spiritual ability. The spiritually gifted may have no sense of God. The Bible gives us examples of people who were greatly used by God but were not *godly*. It also tells us that even people who have performed miracles in Jesus' name will not be saved if they do not personally know Jesus. Character is what counts, not spiritual expertise.

2. When we are motivated by authentic spirituality, our goal is Jesus. We are not interested in *experiences* but in Jesus himself. He captivates our hearts. He is in the center of our vision. Authentic spiritual experience will be satisfied with nothing less.

3. Humility accompanies the presence of God. Having a sense of God's "holy beauty" inevitably creates a sense of our moral and spiritual poverty. We do not know much of true humility in our ambitious society. We tend to think of humility as low self-esteem. But spiritual experience generates real humility: it causes us to forget ourselves and wonder at God.

4. Spirituality is not temporary but causes a permanent change. It does not only last when we are in the mood or in the right settings or under a particular influence. The light of God shines out of the person who knows the presence of God. This is because they have "become like little suns, partaking of the nature of the fountain of light."

5. False spirituality embraces Jesus' salvation only as a license to do wrong. It uses forgiveness to indulge in sinfulness. But authentic spiritual experience does not. True spirituality sees forgiveness as a way to be set free from sin, not to keep on sinning. It does not rejoice in wrong but in good.

6. True knowledge of the presence of God will not be purely cerebral. It will result in right action. Edwards considers this to be the most important sign, "the chief sign of all the signs of grace." When we have encountered the love of God, we shall love others in return. When God has forgiven us, we shall forgive others. When we have received from God, we shall give. When God has served us, we too shall serve.

TWO PATTERNS OF AUTHENTIC SPIRITUAL EXPERIENCE

Edwards recorded the following example of what he took to be an excellent spiritual experience:

> The person, more than once continuing for five or six hours together, without an interruption, in that clear and lively view or sense of the infinite beauty and amiableness of Christ's person and the heavenly sweetness of his excellent and transcendent love; so that (to use the person's own expressions) the soul remained in a kind of heavenly Elysium, and did as it were swim in the rays of Christ's love, like a little mote swimming in the beams of sun, or streams of his light that came in at a window . . . extraordinary views of divine things, and religious affections, being frequently attended with very great effects on the body, nature often sinking under the weight of divine discoveries, the strength of the body was taken away, so as to deprive of all ability to stand or speak; sometimes the hands clinched, and the flesh cold, but senses still remaining; animal nature often in a great emotion and agitation, and the soul very often, of late, so overcome with great admiration, and a kind of omnipotent joy, as to cause the person (wholly unavoidably) to leap with all the might, with joy and mighty exultation of soul. [10]

Listen to Edwards as he concludes a sermon on spiritual experience:

---

10. *Works of Jonathan Edwards, vol. 4, Some Thoughts Concerning the Revival,* Yale University Press, p332.

You tell me that your spiritual experience was definitely something extraordinary. You say it was something beyond your own power to bring about. But my question now is whether you are changed. You can change your mind and change your feelings but still not change yourself. Extraordinary experiences won't necessarily change you anymore than putting on a new shirt changes you. Or anymore than going into a new room. Or listening to a new tune. Or hearing a new story. The Question is not whether you have met with something new but whether you are new. [11]

DEISTS AND ENTHUSIASTS TODAY

The dangers of deism and enthusiasm are very much with us today. There are still those who reject all experience of God as fanatical. There are also fanatics who endorse wild spirituality. And churches are far from immune to such extremes. In fact, I am quite sure that most churches tend strongly to one or other danger. I know churches scared stiff of profound life-changing spiritual experience. I also know churches enthralled with misguided spirituality. To a very large degree this split in Christendom is a reflection of our Enlightenment heritage. We lean toward one or other extreme because our whole intellectual framework is caught on the horns of a dilemma. Our society is straddled between emotionalism and rationalism. Something of a new approach to these matters may be currently emerging in the West. The problem of "modernism" is, some think, being replaced by "postmodernism." That change could provide an opportunity to rethink our approach to spirituality. It could be an open door for us to find a more biblical, a more Christian, spirituality. Here Edwards' approach has much to commend it. He stood at the crossroads of our modern society and called it back to the Bible. As "modernism" runs its course, we may be able to hear his voice with clarity once more. If so, the ghosts of Christian deism and Christian enthusiasm could be laid to rest.

---

11. Beinecke Rare Book and Manuscript Library, Yale University. (Unpublished sermon, preached March 1747.)

CONCLUSION

THE KEY TO KNOWLEDGE

. . . you have taken away the key to knowledge.
Luke 11:52

18

IT'S ALL ABOUT GOD

Imagine you are eavesdropping on a conversation. Three people are sitting at the table next to yours in a coffee shop, discussing God.

The first person says, "I have come across many different kinds of 'spiritual experience.' But I don't know which of them is genuine, and even if I did I wouldn't know how to have that genuine spirituality."

The second person replies, "Well, I don't think we can even talk in terms of 'genuine' spiritual experience. There are too many different kinds of spirituality for that. I think they are all intriguing but none of them can be 'genuine.'"

The third says, "You're both living in cloud-cuckoo-land. I wouldn't mind a "spiritual experience," but how can there be spiritual experiences when we all know that there is no spiritual realm? God is dead."

These are representative citizens of our changing world, each living in one of the three different lands identified at the start of this book. The first occupies the land called confusion. The second dwells where gods are fashionable. The third inhabits a place where God is considered to be dead.

Many of us do not really want to play the part of any of the three people in that conversation. We would like to find solid ground in the spiritual, a way to know God's presence; we would like to not feel "lost." The guide to authentic spirituality that we have outlined in this book could show us how to find our way. It tells us that true spiritual experience is discovered in the gospel of Jesus Christ, by faith, through revelation, producing godliness. There is a way to know the presence of God. There is a way to rejoice in him. There is a way to be certain of our spirituality. There is a way to know for sure that God exists, that God loves us, and wants us and cares for us. We can experience authentic spirituality; we can experience his presence in our lives day by day.

Wherever we are in our spiritual lives, we can take the next step along the way. What will a journey down the path of knowing the presence of God entail?

For some it will mean going to church regularly. True spiritual experience is personal but it is not solitary. Advertisements and contemporary culture encourage us to think and act as an individual. But as we travel along the road to God, we shall meet other people journeying with us. God's people walk in community, in the church. Here there are people from different classes, different races, different ages, different accents, different cultures, and with different personalities. Some are old, some are young, some are wealthy, some are poor, some are married and some are single. This diversity is one of the most rewarding parts of being in a church. It is also one of the most challenging. In the Christian community we rub shoulders with people who are not like us. We choose our friends but we do not choose our family, it is said. Similarly, church is a family not a social club of friends. This makes it a rainbow community, sparkling with all the colors and variety of the human race. It also makes it complicated. But ideally the family works together supporting each other and encouraging each other to make the most of all that God has given each person.

For others the next step will mean continuing to wrestle with some of the issues that spirituality raises. There are more questions about authentic spirituality and knowing the presence of God than this book can answer. Asking questions is OK. Being a "seeker" of spiritual experience is all right as long as we do not become an addict of spiritual experiences (in the plural), or someone who is happier looking than finding. Perhaps you could pray (again) about the issues that still perplex you. Perhaps you could look in more detail at some of the Bible passages we studied. Do not give up. There is an element of continual questioning and seeking in real faith; but there can also be an element of satisfied resolution. Jesus does not answer all our questions in this life, but he is the answer. The more we get to know him personally the more what we do not understand becomes clearer or less important.

There may also be those who will want to work out how authentic spirituality could reform the institutions of the church. Four areas, I believe, need to be investigated.

1. Preaching

Some people today say that preaching is out of date. They say that it is conceited for a person to stand in a pulpit and "preach at" others. We should dialogue and discuss truth—it should not be proclaimed. Besides, they also say, we live in a time of image not of word when people watch TV and do not read books. I am, though, unconvinced. I am unconvinced partly because people have always said that preaching is out of date. There is no golden age of preaching when everyone thought preaching was a good thing. Preaching has always come under attack. But I am also unconvinced because preaching is not lecturing. It is an avenue of spiritual experience. Certainly, preaching is teaching, as the Bible tells us. But this teaching is not simply educational. A person teaching the Bible hopes to be a vehicle for knowing God's presence. It is a divine encounter.

2. Apologetics

Apologetics is what people do when they reason for the truth of Christianity. There are three approaches to apologetics. Some advance "evidences" for Christianity. Others engage some people's beliefs or "worldviews" and attempt to expose their inconsistency in comparison to the coherence of the Christian worldview. And still others think that any kind of apologetics is compromise with worldly reason and should be avoided. We may have some sympathy with all three approaches. Our world's reason does sometimes smack too much of human pride. Why should God be held to the bar of our finite mind? Yet we dare not suggest that God is irrational. There is evidence for Christianity. There is coherence to the Christian worldview. Our particular contribution to reasoning the truth of Christianity is twofold. First, it is to demonstrate the normality of "faith-reason." God asks us to believe him for the same sort of reasons that we ask people to trust us. Second, it is to establish the significance of the concept of Christian revelation. This historical revelation of God in Christ stands above all other claims to religious revelations. The twofold contribution may lead to the formation of "revelation apologetics," reasoning from faith on the basis of revelation, and a distinctly scriptural approach to engagement with the world.

3. Living

Talk is cheap. Thought is no good if it does not lead to action. Truth is meaningless if it cannot be lived. Knowing the presence of God should lead to practicing the presence of God, to living each day in the light of God's truth. This is the constant burden of the New Testament Epistles. They do not say, "Live the life;" they do not say, "Think the truth"; instead, they say, "Live the truth." True truth produces real action. Knowing the presence of God should influence our behavior in several ways. It should make us hunger for the Word. It should make us long to obey Jesus. It should make us consciously depend upon the Holy Spirit. It should help us to live as God wants, at home, at work, and as a church. Centering upon God's Word, prioritizing Jesus, relying on the Holy Spirit: these are three models of spirituality which will form our practice. By them we might want to construct a spiritual audit of our practice. We could ask ourselves questions about each aspect of spirituality. Do we act according to our understanding of God's Word? Do we allow God's voice to speak though his Word by giving quality time to its study, both on our own and as a church? Do we prioritize the message of the cross of Jesus in our speaking about God? Do we repent of our sins and bring them to the cross for forgiveness? Do we ignore the Spirit and act as if we did not need him? Do we ask for God's Spirit to help us to live the truth?

4. Dying

We seldom think about it, for often enough we are at least scared of the process if not the actual experience of death. We make macabre jokes about it. But, unless Christ returns first, we all will need to come face to face with the "last enemy," death. One of the great signs of a genuine spirituality, and our progress in knowing more about God and his presence in our lives, is a strength in the face of great suffering, and even death. Because many of our religious leaders only wish to say things that will appear positive, our generation has not received much teaching on the subject of death. We are robbed. Our faith is in Christ who died and rose again. We are not scared of the graveside. We are not surprised by suffering. We believe in the God who has scars on his hands. And as such our great hope is a hope that has victory over pain, suffering, and, yes, even death.

5. Revival

We have seen that there are good and bad understandings of revival. At its best revival is a sense of the presence of God. He seems more real, more evident, more apparent. People wake up to God's awesome purity. People wake up to God's endless love. People wake up to God's reality. He exists, he lives, he saves, he "is," here and now. This is the experience of revival. The effects of revival can be diverse, depending on the subjects of the experience, the tenor of the times and the wisdom and sensibility of the leaders. But its experience is always this blinding knowledge of the presence of God. Bad understandings of revival turn people away from emotional engagement with God. They fear manipulation. If there were one result of this book that I would crave it would be a deep desire for people to seek the knowledge of God's presence. Structures come and structures go, but unless God grants us a reviving knowledge of his presence our efforts will be in vain. Perhaps you can be a part of God's reviving work by seeking to know and make known the presence of God.

The world is constantly changing. Trying to pin it down is like trying to stop time. Tomorrow it will be different. New fads, new fashions, new ideas, new currents in the cultural climate constantly emerge. This flux is symptomatic of a world running out of steam. The sand in the hourglass is emptying. As we view our changing world, our hope for the future rests not in an idea or a person or an answer, but in an unchanging God. When we think about knowing the presence of God, it is essential that we finish with God and not with ourselves. Nothing could be further from authentic spiritual experience than that which is satisfied with it. We shall find our greatest security in giving God the last word. To know even something of the presence of God means a taste of God. Knowing his presence is not *knowing* his presence, or even knowing his *presence*: it is knowing *his* presence. We are fascinated neither by the possibility of knowledge, nor by the experience of his presence. If we have any knowledge of his presence, we are captivated by him.

Breinigsville, PA USA
06 October 2010

246796BV00002B/59/P